bloom

bloom

a memoir

KELLE HAMPTON

WILLIAM MORROW

An Imprint of HarperCollinsPublishers

Designed by Lorie Pagnozzi

Library of Congress Cataloging-in-Publication Data

Hampton, Kelle.
  Bloom: finding beauty in the unexpected—a memoir / Kelle Hampton. — 1st ed.
    p. cm.
  ISBN 978-0-06-204503-4
  1. Parents of children with disabilities. 2. Down syndrome. 3. Mothers and daughters. 4. Children with disabilities—Family relationships. I. Title.
  HQ773.7.H25 2012
  305.9'084092—dc23
  [B]

2011024788

---

12 13 14 15 16   OV/QGT   10 9 8 7 6 5

For Lainey.

WHO SHOWED ME HOW TO LOVE

"Tell me, what is it you plan to do with your one wild and precious life?"

—mary oliver

contents

Prologue: The Story of Nella's Birth 1

CHAPTER 1: waiting   21

CHAPTER 2: home   41

CHAPTER 3: room 16   57

CHAPTER 4: the blue pill   75

CHAPTER 5: homecoming   91

CHAPTER 6: new life   109

CHAPTER 7: week one   125

CHAPTER 8: moving on   141

CHAPTER 9: blueprint   159

CHAPTER 10: support   177

CHAPTER 11: the current   197

CHAPTER 12: jeremy   213

CHAPTER 13: nella's rockstars   235

CHAPTER 14: becoming real   251

Acknowledgments 275

nella's
birth

I TURNED THIRTY-ONE ON DECEMBER 29, 2009. MY husband and I went to dinner with friends the evening before, and as we left, toting our leftovers in Styrofoam boxes and marveling at my very round pregnant belly that seemed to have grown a bit since dinner, I noticed the welcoming glow of the nearby bookstore. I had told Brett I didn't need anything this year for my birthday, since Christmas had just passed and we had splurged on a new lens for my camera, but at the sight of the store window, I remembered a book that had been recommended by another photographer. As we walked by, I told Brett I changed my mind. I wanted that book, and I needed it that very second. So we ventured in, and he played downstairs with our two-year-old, Lainey, while I wandered up in the self-help section, thumbing through titles until I landed on the only copy—*A Million Miles in a Thousand Years* by Donald Miller.

Later at home, we put Lainey to bed and I drew a bath and climbed in, heaving my round middle over the edge of the tub and sinking into warm suds with my new book and a highlighter in hand. And I read. And read. And read. Underlining, highlighting, starring paragraphs and quotes and words that moved me hard. I warmed the water about a trillion times and pruned my skin to raisins, but I could not stop reading. I passed three hours in that tub, followed by another hour or so of reading in my bed.

The book spoke of the power of challenges—how living a life of comfort does nothing to make us grow, and how hard times shape us into interesting, developed characters. By the end of the book, I was inspired. Inspired to write a new story for our life—inspired to face challenges and leave my comfort zone and go through hard things because that is what turns the screenplays of our lives from boring to Oscar-worthy. And to be honest, in my mind, our most uncomfortable challenge boiled down to one thing: the changes in our life with Brett's job and having him away from home. Little did I know.

Fast-forward.

Three weeks later, a Thursday, Brett and I teased all day that we were so ready for this baby, she had to either come Thursday or Friday. Every time he called me from work, he told me I should be out *jogging*. I didn't jog, but I did walk like crazy, trailing Lainey through the streets of our neighborhood in a stroller, thinking, *These might be the last moments with my only daughter alone.*

Thursday night, the pains started coming—nothing horribly uncomfortable but some significant cramps that were semiregular and popped up several times through the night. By morning, I had several that were fifteen to twenty minutes apart, and my doctor, convinced I would go fast once I was in full swing, suggested I go to the hospital within a few hours. I remember getting off the phone and it hit me: today was going to be the day. It was surreal. I texted my friends, called my family, began the last steps in the long process of saying good-bye to my *only child*. She wanted her face painted like a kitty, and although I was excited to pack

up and head to the hospital, I savored every brushstroke of those last moments with my big girl.

I called my friend Katie in Fort Lauderdale. Katie was the delivery nurse the night Lainey was born, and we have since been forever friends. She promised me she wanted to be present for all my babies' births, so she hightailed it over I-75 after my call to get there in time.

It was strange. It seemed so real and yet I had dreamed of this moment for so long, it was almost like a dream itself: Wanting a second child. Losing a pregnancy. Getting pregnant. The horrible night I thought it was all ending and the trip to the ER where we saw that little heartbeat. Waiting and preparing and finally, these last weeks, having everything just—*perfect*. The birth music ready to go, the blankets I had made packed and ready, the coming-home outfit, the big sister crown for Lainey, the nightgown I had bought just for the occasion—what I would wear holding my daughter the first night I rocked her to sleep. Even the favors I hand-designed and tied every ribbon to were lined and stacked in a box, ready to pass out the moment the room flooded with visitors. My heart could hardly hold the excitement, and I will never ever forget what it feels like to long for your baby to be placed in your arms the last few days of your pregnancy—it's so real, you can touch it.

We said good-bye to Lainey as we left her with Grandma and headed to the hospital, where I was quickly instructed in Room 7 to drop trou and gown up. I slipped my white ruffled skirt and black shirt into a plastic belongings bag. Days later, just the sight of these clothes—the ones I wore during all the excitement, during those last *happy* moments before my life was changed—would bring pain. I think my friend Heidi finally hid the bag because it made me cry every time.

The early stages of labor were perfectly beautiful. Nothing hurt that bad, I had the anticipation of this utopian experience ahead of me, Brett was chill, and my girlfriends started trickling in the room. We actually played a game—the "If you could" cards I had packed in my bag for this very purpose. *If you could vacation to anywhere in the world, where would it be? If you could change one thing about your past, what would it be?* I played moderator, firing questions from my hospital bed—questions that ignited good conversation, laughter, the feeling that this was fun

and beautiful and more like a sleepover than an afternoon hooked up to monitors and IVs. And all the while, among the laughter and small talk was the accompanying melody of the girl I was about to meet. Her heart steadily beat a beautiful rhythm that could be heard loud and clear from the monitor strapped to my middle. *Bum-pum. Bum-pum. Bum-pum.* I had it perfectly planned, and it was going just as I had imagined—but *better.*

By 2:00, my water had broken and my contractions were in full force. The room was full of excitement and laughter. I chatted with my girl-friends until a contraction came on where I shifted gears, *"ow-ow-ow-ow-ow'd"* my way through it (and cursed), and came out of it as fast as I went in, picking up the conversation where we left off. I checked to make sure Brett was okay. Several of my girlfriends were headed out to a birthday party but, with news of my status, they all huddled into the room, dressed to the nines, to check on me before their night out. I liked the commotion. I loved the anticipation. I loved the feeling of people waiting anxiously for *our baby.* It felt special . . . and we were so ready.

Two hours went by and I was off the wall in pain, begging for anes-thesia to get in with an epidural. They were tied up, and so I cursed them, too. Little did I know, I was dilated to nine centimeters. This is where things begin to get hazy. It all just happened so fast. I remember anes-thesia walking in to give me an epidural, Brett getting uneasy, girlfriends talking me through it, my pediatrician stopping in to say hi during her rounds, and my obstetrician walking in and gowning up. This was it. With Lainey, it took forever, and here I was, just hours after walking into this place, and they were going to tell me to push. They were going to tell me "just one more," and then suddenly my life was going to change.

I couldn't grasp it even then. It was all just happening so fast and I wanted to savor it. I looked around the room and tried to take it in—the candles, the music, the lavender oil I brought that wafted through the room and calmed the tension. And then I remember just speaking to my-self. *You are about to meet your daughter. You are about to be changed for good.*

At this moment, I heard the sounds of our birth song begin to fill the room . . . "When You Love Someone." And I began to cry. My hus-

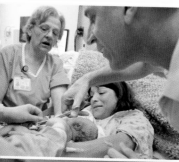

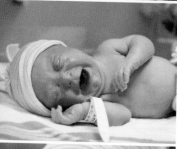

band, my friends, my dad, my nurses . . . all of them smiling . . . cameras flashing . . .

One more push.

Oh, this is so hard . . .

I pushed. I pushed and watched as the tiniest little body came out of me, arms flailing, lungs wailing . . . and then, they put her in my arms.

. . . and I knew.

I knew the minute I saw her that she had Down syndrome and nobody else knew. I held her and cried. Cried and panned the room to meet eyes with anyone who would tell me she didn't have it. I held her and looked at her like she wasn't my baby and tried to take it in. And all I can remember of these moments is her face. I will never forget my daughter in my arms, opening her eyes over and over . . . she locked eyes with mine and stared . . . bore holes into my soul.

Love me. Love me. I'm not what you expected, but oh, please love me.

That was the most defining moment of my life. That was the beginning of my story.

I don't remember a lot here. My friends have filled me in, but I feel like I was in a black hole. I know I held her. I know I kissed her. I know I begged every power in the world that this wasn't happening, that she was normal, that I would wake up and be pregnant again. But I knew in my soul exactly what this was.

She was scooped off my chest and taken to the warming bed where nurses nervously smiled as they checked her over. I wanted someone to tell me what was going on. I kept asking if she was okay, and they told me she was fine. She was crying and pink and just perfectly healthy. I wanted to say the words, but couldn't. So I asked why her nose was smoothed, why she looked funny. And because she came out posterior and so quickly, many people in the room honestly thought she'd look a little different in an hour or so. But I knew. I cried while everyone smiled and took pictures of her, like nothing was wrong. I kept crying and asking, "Is there something you aren't telling me?" . . . and they just kept smiling.

At this point, I had believed the pediatrician came in right away and told me the news. But because I was so confused and emotional, I am told it wasn't right away. The nurses apparently called my pediatrician in for "DS suspicions," and during this hour, I was handed back my daughter as if everything was okay.

When I've thought about this time later, I've cried and cringed, wondering what I did. Did she feel love? Did I kiss her? Did I hold her and tell her *happy birthday* and smother her with happy tears? My friends who were in the room smile when I ask this and promise me I did. They tell me I couldn't stop kissing her. And while I held her, the room went on. Someone popped champagne and poured glasses and a toast was

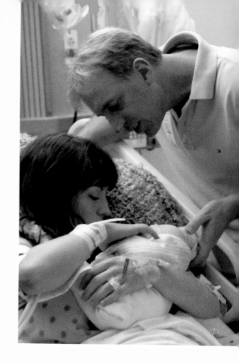

raised. "To Nella!" they cheered, while I sat, confused, trying to take it in.

I remember feeling . . . *nothing*. As if I literally left my body for a bit. But they said I kissed her. They said I loved her. They said I was a mama.

Suddenly, my pediatrician walked in, and my heart sank. This was it.

"Why is she here?" I asked. They told me she was just checking the baby out, which she did. And then the room grew quiet and everyone was asked to leave. I started shaking. I knew it was coming. The tears. The twisting in my stomach as they were about to rock my world.

Brett stood behind me, stroking my hair, and my nurse friends, Dot and Katie, stayed on either side of the bed. And it happened.

My pediatrician snuggled Nella up in a blanket and handed her to me, and she knelt down next to my bed so that she could look up at me— not down. She smiled so warmly and held my hand so tight. And she never took her eyes off mine. We had been through a lot together with Lainey's jaundice, and I had spent many tearful conversations with her over the course of these two and a half years. She is an amazing pediatrician, but at this moment, she became more than that. She was our friend as she beautifully shared the news.

I need to tell you something.

. . . and I cried hard . . . "I know what you're going to say."

She smiled again and squeezed my hand a little tighter.

The first thing I'm going to tell you is that your daughter is beautiful and perfect.

. . . and I cried harder.

. . . *but there are some features that lead me to believe she may have Down syndrome.*

Finally, someone said it.

I felt hot tears stream down and fall on my baby's face. My beautiful, perfect daughter. I was scared to look up at Brett, so I didn't. I just kissed her.

And then, Dr. Foley added . . .

. . . *but, Kelle, she is beautiful. And perfect.*

I suddenly remembered my dad was in the hallway. He had been in the delivery room just minutes earlier wearing the "Poppa" shirt he had made for this special occasion, smiling and cheering as she entered the world and now I had to tell him what I knew. I felt like a child again—needy and vulnerable. I wanted my dad. I wanted my mom. I wanted my brother and sister by my side. I asked for my dad to be let back in the room, and when he walked in, I cried again. "Dad, they think she has Down syndrome."

He smiled genuinely as his eyes welled up with tears. "That's okay. We love her." He scooped her up, and I asked him to say a prayer. And there, in the delivery room where moments earlier she entered the world, we huddled around my bed—Brett still stroking my hair, Katie crying on one side, Dot on the other, and Dr. Foley kneeling down beside my bed. Dad prayed and thanked God for giving us Nella and thanked him for the wonderful things he had planned for us. For our family. For Nella. Amen.

As soon as my dad finished, I looked up at him, completely desperate and flailing. "I need Carin. Now." My sister was my rock, and her presence was imperative for my moving forward. He assured me she'd be on a flight the next day, and my mom would follow.

Dr. Foley hugged me and told me she got to hold Nella for her examination, but now she wanted to hold her just for some snuggles. And she did. I will always remember her compassion and know there is no one else who could have supported us in the kind and confident way she did.

Katie asked if I wanted to nurse Nella, another dreamy moment I had long anticipated. Yet it felt so different this time. I remember her latch-

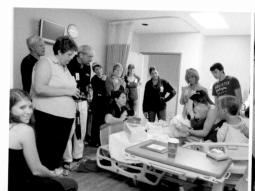

ing right on and sucking away with no hesitation, completely accepting me as her mama and snuggling in to the only one she's ever known—and I felt so completely guilty that I didn't feel the same. I felt love, yes. I just kept envisioning this other baby—the one I felt had died the moment I realized she wasn't what I expected. But the nursing—oh, the nursing—how incredibly bonding it was. The single most beautiful link I had to falling in love with this blessed angel.

The hallway was still filled with visitors—and there are stories from our other wonderful friends and family about what happened behind those walls while they waited. All I know is that there was more love in that birthing center than the place could hold. As anxious eyes reentered the room, I held my baby and told them all, crying, what we had been told. I knew there was a stream of friends ready to come and celebrate and I wanted them all to be told before they came in. I couldn't emotionally handle telling anyone and yet, strangely, I wanted people to know as soon as possible because I knew I needed the troops. I was falling, sliding, tunneling into a black hole; and I needed as much love as possible to keep me up.

I just remember happiness. From everyone. All the amazing souls in that room celebrated as if there was nothing but joy. Everyone knew—and there were a few puffy eyes—but mostly, it was pure happiness. More friends trickled in. More smiles. More toasts. And hugs with no words—hugs like I've never felt. Ones that spoke volumes—arms pulled tightly around my neck, lips pressed against my forehead, and bodies that shook with sobs—sobs that told me they felt it too. They felt my pain and they wanted to take it away.

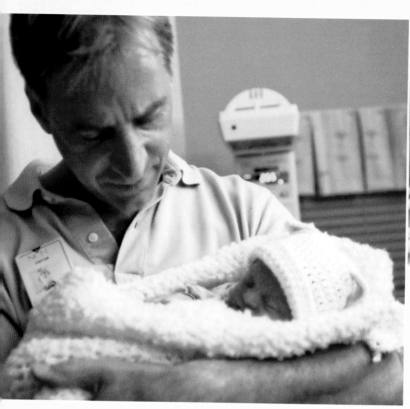
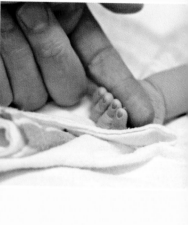

And Brett . . . well, he never left our girl's side. He was quiet through this all, and I'm not sure I'll ever know what he felt, but I know the daddy of our babies, and I know he knows nothing but to love them with all his heart. And he did so from the very beginning.

As soon as the epidural wore off, I wanted my own nightgown. They were going to take me to our new room upstairs, and I was ready for a new start. Everyone carried our stuff up and waited for us. And then . . . the moment I always talked about—the moment they put you in that wheelchair and place the baby in your arms . . . and stroll you through the hallways to your room while onlookers smile and wish they were you. It's so strange, but I barely remember it.

I remember arriving to our room and being told Lainey was on her way. And I cried new tears. I hadn't even thought about how this would impact Lainey, what she would think, how her life would be different, how every beautiful vision I had of two sisters growing up together— grown-up phone calls, advice giving, cooking together, shopping—

everything would be different. Numbness started leaving my heart, and sheer pain settled in.

Don't cry. Don't cry. Don't cry when Lainey gets here.

. . . and then I'll never forget her face . . . her cute outfit someone put her in . . . her eyes when she walked into that room, and the way she tried to hide her excitement with her shy smile.

I will never forget the day my girl became a big sister.

I will never forget the moment her little sister was placed in her arms. I watched in agony . . . in tears . . . in admiration as my little girl taught me how to love. She showed me what unconditional love looks like . . . what the absence of stereotypes feels like . . . she was . . . proud.

. . . and that was one of the most beautiful moments of my life. I *needed* that.

As darkness set in that night and people started trickling out, I felt paranoid. So completely afraid because I knew with darkness, with the absence of everyone celebrating, that grief would come. I could feel it coming, and it hurt so, so, so very bad.

I wanted Lainey to go home with Brett. My heart was in a million pieces and wanted to be with her, and if I couldn't, I wanted him there. And so he left, with the little girl who completed my world, while I remained in the hospital with my two amazing, wonderful friends, Heidi and Katie, who will never ever know how special they are because of what they did for me that night. They heard and saw things no one else will ever know, but I could have never made it through the night without them.

I think I cried for seven hours straight. It was gut-wrenching pain. I held Nella and I kissed her, but I literally writhed in emotional pain on that bed in the dark with our candles and my friends by my side until the sun came up. I remember trying to sleep and then feeling it come on again, and I'd start shaking, and they'd both jump up and hug me from either side, Nella smooshed between the three of us. I begged for morning, even once mistaking a streetlamp for the sun and turning on the lights only to find it was 3:00 A.M. and I still had to make it through the night.

"This isn't happening," I moaned. "Please make it go away. I want to wake up. Oh, please let me wake up." And Katie would stroke my hair and Heidi would bury her head into my shoulder and both of them would whisper over and over, "You're going to be okay, Kelle. You're going to be okay. We're not leaving you."

I CAN'T EXPLAIN THAT EVENING. I SUPPOSE IT'S HORRIBLE to say you spent the first night your daughter was born in that state of agony, but I know it was necessary for me to move on to where I am today. And, knowing where I am today and how much I love this soul, how much I know she was meant for me and I am meant for her, knowing the crazy way our souls have intertwined and grown into each other, I can say all this now. It's hard, but it's real, and we all have feelings. We live them, we breathe them, we go through them, and soon they dissolve into new feelings. So here I go.

I cried out that I wanted to leave her and run away. I wanted to take Lainey and my perfect world and this perfect love I had built with my two-year-old and our cupcake-baking days and our art projects and our beautiful bond and I wanted to run like hell. I wanted to be pregnant again. I wanted to be pregnant so bad. I wanted it to be the morning Nella was born, when I was happy and excited and when I wore the white ruffled skirt and black shirt and put it in the belongings bag knowing joy was to come. I wanted to go back. I wanted to go back. I wanted to go back.

I moaned in pain and through it all, this little breath of heaven needed me. I cried while I nursed her. I cried while I held her. I cried while I pulled my nightgown off just so I could lay her body on my naked skin and pray that I felt a bond. I writhed in emotional torment for hours, and Heidi and Katie saw parts of me no one else has ever seen. My eyes were so swollen, Heidi said I looked like Rocky, like someone beat the hell out of my face and then cut little slits for eyes. It was that bad.

And then morning came, and with it, hope.

My sister arrived and revolutionized the place with her own version of an "I Have a Dream" speech. She told me I swallowed the blue pill. She told me I could never go back, but that I held a key to a door that no one else does. With tears in her eyes, she excitedly and passionately told me how lucky I was. She told me that I was chosen and that it would be the most special thing in the world. She told me it was going to be just fine.

And she was so right.

The day after Nella was born, I fell in love hard. I knew she was mine. I knew we were destined to be together. I knew she was the baby all along that grew in my beautiful round tummy, the one I thought I almost lost, the one that I proudly rubbed when people told me how beautiful that belly was. *It was.* It was Nella all along.

Over the course of the next several days, things just became beautiful. I cried, yes, but they soon turned to tears of joy. I felt lucky. I felt happy. I felt like I didn't want to run away with Lainey anymore—and if I did, I was taking my bunny with me.

When Lainey was in the hospital with jaundice, I remember hugging Brett and crying. I told him if God would make her better, I'd do anything. I'd live in a box, I'd sell everything we had, I'd be happy with nothing—just make her better. When she did get better, that feeling of raw gratitude was real, but it wasn't long before real life set in and I was complaining once again about the dirty grout in our cheap tile and how much I wanted wood floors.

I've often thought about how quickly that feeling left because we have a perfect, healthy little girl running around who erases all the painful memories of when we thought something might be seriously wrong.

I felt that feeling again with Nella. And as the pain has slowly dissipated, I've realized that I will always be reminded. My Nella, my special little bunny, my beautiful *perfect* yet unique girl will be my constant reminder in life. That it's not about wood floors. No, life is about love and truly experiencing the beauty we are meant to know.

And so, we came home . . . *happy*. In fact, walking out of the hospital with our new baby girl and our proud new big girl, all crowned up, gripping the handle of the car seat with Daddy, it *was* just how I had imagined it.

Life moves on. There have been lots of tears since and there will be more. But there is *us. Our Family.* We will embrace this beauty and make something of it. We will hold our precious gift and know that we are lucky. I *feel* lucky. I feel privileged. I feel there is a plan so beautiful in store . . . and we get to live it. Wow.

The story has begun . . .

chapter 1
waiting

IT WAS TWO DAYS BEFORE LAINEY'S FIRST BIRTHDAY when Brett finally gave in and agreed that we could try for another baby. I had longed for one since the day Lainey grew out of the light blue cotton sleeper with the pink strawberries on it that I associated with every ounce of newborn-ness she possessed. And at that party, as we watched our little girl blow out her candle and smear white frosting all over her cheeks in celebration of that first astounding year of life, I was comforted by the fact that the sadness I felt surrounding her getting older would soon be replaced by the joy of knowing another "little" was on the way.

But it didn't happen. I had gotten pregnant with Lainey within two months, so by the fourth month of trying for my second baby, I grew impatient. I also understood how annoying it must be for women who struggle with infertility when the onslaught of sympathetic advice pours in. *It'll happen. When you relax. When Brett's job stress is gone. When you're not thinking about it. When you try Clomid. When you're least expecting it. Blah, blah, blah.*

The thing was, I didn't want to wait. I could taste her then. What she looked like. What she smelled like. What the weight of her tiny body felt like in my arms. I yearned for another baby as if the survival of the human race depended on it, and if I had to pee on a stick one more time and squint my eyes searching for a line that didn't exist, I thought I'd pretty much die.

Which is why, on March 9, 2009, after quite a bit of anticipation, I jumped around the kitchen sobbing and screaming holding a pregnancy test with two pink lines. Two. After eleven and a half boxes of pregnancy tests over the previous months and all the imaginary second lines I had conjured up in my brain, I finally saw a real one. It was beautiful . . . and exciting. It held the promise of another amazing journey I was already blessed to know so well.

I'm not sure when my mother heart was born, but for as long as I can remember, I've wanted kids. Forty-seven of 'em, to be exact, and I used to tell people I was going to marry my dad and raise those kids in a tree house in the backyard. That wasn't exactly feasible for a number of reasons (legality and morality chief among them), but at least I had some ambitious goals at a young age. My mom tells me I wanted a job in the church nursery when I was six and that my scrawny body could carry a tot on my hip like I had been doing it for years. Even my first kindergarten paper—an "All About Me" assignment that came home in my backpack that first day of school—bore proof of my destiny. Under where I had filled in "pizza" for my favorite food and "Buffy" for the family dog, there was a line of red Crayola chicken-scratched letters in all caps— a forceful answer to *What do you want to be when you grow up?* **A MOM.** And, at the ripe old age of eight, I spent many afternoons lying on the living room carpet of my best friend's house where we rifled through old baby photos from our family albums, pretended we were the moms, and wrote our fake kids' names in Magic Marker, along with all the activities they were involved in on the back. I recently found one of my own baby pictures and flipped it over to find my eight-year-old handwriting: *"Nicole Alexandra. Ballet. Tennis. Soccer."*

Life, of course, didn't turn out exactly as I'd planned it. My sister had her kids well before me, and I lived vicariously through her for many years. I skipped so many classes my first year of college to be with my nieces that I actually had to retake Psychology and Microbiology. If it wasn't for the fact that I finally moved away from her to finish school, I'd probably be living alone, attending my nieces' parent-teacher conferences today. Not to mention I'd be well versed in psychology and microbiology.

Eventually, I had to cut the cord, so to speak. I packed up my teal Ford Escort station wagon with a few pieces of clothing and a hundred framed pictures of my nieces, made my tearful good-byes, and drove the great distance of 120 miles to Spring Arbor, Michigan. I needed to finish school and find myself. Finish school, I did, but find myself, not so much.

Spring Arbor University is a small, faith-based college known for bestowing upon its graduates not only a valuable degree, but also a devoted spouse. Most of my friends met and married their fellow classmates there, planning their weddings in between taking notes in the basement of the Whiteman-Gibbs Science Building. I, on the other hand, didn't meet anyone. I graduated after four years with a diploma in one hand and a prescription for Zoloft in the other. I had gained the "fresh-man fifteen" plus another five or so every following year. I didn't know what I wanted to do with my life, I couldn't find a permanent teaching job, and living with my dad wasn't exactly the Chicago studio bachelorette pad I had dreamed of. I was dressed and ready for life but had nowhere to go.

I spent a year postcollege as a substitute teacher at two elementary schools, all the while watching my friends start their lives and wondering what I was going to do with mine. I was a damn good teacher and poured myself into my sub jobs, even offering to do lesson plans and grading for other teachers when I could. I felt like I had so many ideas, so much energy, so much creativity and love built up, but no outlet, nowhere to use it. So I delivered a social studies lesson to a fourth-grade class like my life depended on it. I dressed up like Christopher Columbus. I brought in samples of exotic teas to make the Boston Tea Party lesson a little more fun. Heck, I once set up an entire grocery store in a classroom with canned goods and a cash register to teach a math lesson. I even had my local grocery store make me a real name tag. But still, I didn't belong. I wanted my own classroom. My own place. My own family. My own life. I was tired of living through everyone else, and I needed a jump start to shake things up.

Finally, a year later, I accepted a teaching job in Naples, Florida, on a whim after a fifteen-minute phone interview. At the time, I was doing odd jobs in the hospital Cardiology Department where my dad was a chaplain, and I'll never forget hanging up the phone in his office on my lunch break, after I got hired. My dad walked in to find me sitting there at his desk, crying in my blue scrubs. "I have a job, Dad. In Naples. And my first day of school is in eleven days."

And so I packed up and marked the beginning of my new life by saying good-bye to my teal station wagon, which had by now acquired a duct-taped fender, a dented passenger door, and a push button starter. In its place, I bought a Chevy Malibu—splurged on a new car but scrimped on roll-down windows. It was black and sleek and represented a new start.

I arrived in Naples feeling invigorated, courageous, and spontaneous. Which is why I enjoyed the span of very *unmotherly* behavior that followed—behavior that may or may not have included falling off a six-foot amp in a Miami club where I was dancing some very cool moves. I'll never know what happened to the guy I landed on, but I do know that I was carried out with a smile on my face and woke up six hours later in a bed with an earth-shattering headache. And if my children are reading this, I made that up.

I found a condo and decorated it with an eclectic mix of furnishings from Home Goods and Target that somehow, when put together and re-arranged a few times, eventually resembled a photo spread in *Home Dé-cor,* in my humble opinion. I hung framed covers of vintage *Vogues* on my new yellow walls (*Bagel* yellow, as I recall the paint chip saying) and piled up billiard balls in old vases on my coffee table. It was youthful and swanky and, combined with my new weight loss (finally lost the fresh-man fifteen) and newly acquired running habit, I started to feel kind of cool again—like someone I might want to be friends with. So I started having parties, spending way too much time on hand-sequined invites that said corny things like *Cocktails and Cupcakes at Kelle's,* and passed them out to fellow teachers who actually showed up.

And then I met Brett.

It was totally unplanned, just the way they tell you it's going to hap-pen. Julie, my team leader, walked into my classroom one day, just weeks after I moved, and interrupted my earnest paper grading with a, "Hey, would you ever go out with an older man?"

"Does he have his own teeth and breathe on his own?" I asked. You never know what "older" means when you live in Florida or, as my grandpa called it, Heaven's Waiting Room. But Richard Gere was *older.* George Clooney was *older.* And they were hot. And, according to Julie, so was Brett.

He was divorced, had two boys, and was described by her as "tall, blond, handsome, and an *incredible father.*" She heavily emphasized the last part, dragging out *incredible father* like a Valley girl describing a guy who's *totally hot.* I had nothing to lose. There was something com-pletely intriguing about Brett, the tall, blond, and handsome father, and I wanted to meet him.

Two weeks later, I watched from inside the window of the Mexican restaurant where we met for a group date with friends as Brett tenderly helped his boys climb out of the car and guided them toward the door. He was tall and handsome, just like Julie said, and despite the fact that I hated his shoes (a minor setback that later worked itself out when I took him to Dillard's and introduced him to a man sandal that didn't look like something Jesus would wear), I was smitten. He smiled genuinely, shook my hand, was kind and complimentary, all the while focusing most of his attention on his boys. He stroked his eldest's hair while he laughed at my stories. He cuddled his youngest on his knee as he passed out napkins to our friends and ordered me another beer. I loved that among the awkwardness of us both knowing we were here with all these people to meet each other and form a possible match, he was still an attentive father. His kids came first, and I admired that.

It wasn't long before he was showing up in my classroom on Tuesdays to bring me lunch. And the deal sealer? *He wanted more kids.* We talked about it a lot, having kids. He said he always wanted a daughter, and pointing out little blond girls with pigtails that looked like they could be ours was becoming a favorite pastime. His boys, Austyn and Brandyn, liked me and I liked them. Hell, even his ex-wife and I got along. It was more than perfect. What started as a group date at a Mexican restaurant was turning into something more. For the next three years we dated, and for the first time, I was beginning to find my place. And Hampton sounded like a damn good name to follow Kelle. *Kelle Hampton*. I wrote it with a calligraphy pen in my journal and stared at it. I liked it.

On July 1, 2006, we were married in a little white chapel with our friends and family by our side, and we started trying for a baby soon after. I quit my teaching job, took up photography full-time, and settled into my new life like it was a comfortable chair, just waiting for me to break it in even more. Brett's boys lived half of the week with us and half of the week with their mom, and while our blended family worked out quite swimmingly, I worried a bit when I was trying to get pregnant that my first baby would be Brett's third—a *been-there-done-that* milestone for him—and that consequently his excitement wouldn't rival mine. I was proven wrong the moment I saw his tears when I announced our first baby girl was on her way. Together, we celebrated at every stage of my pregnancy. We held hands the first time we heard her heartbeat, taped ultrasound pictures to the refrigerator, wandered through aisles at Babies "R" Us fighting over who got to "gun down" the bar codes for our baby registry. And we talked about everything. I felt confident that I would be a good mom. And when any fears emerged, I knew the *incredible father* I married would lead the way.

The day we welcomed Lainey Love into our life was nothing short of pure magic, and the next two years with her were beautiful. Don't get me wrong, motherhood is hard. It's scary and trying and demanding. You stretch yourself, learn about yourself, and reach your breaking point, only to come back to that bond—that love that ties you to your *little*. Watching the culmination of your cells, your soul, your personality literally bloom before you, it's just amazing to witness. When Lainey dumped a can of oatmeal on the kitchen floor and waxed the tile with a stick of butter, there was still the way she needed me and nuzzled her head into my neck that outweighed the frustration. When I lost sleep because of frequent feedings or midnight

fevers, there was still the reward of hearing "I love you" for the first time from the little soul who calls me *Mama*. Life is like that though. Every bad thing is tempered by the good, and every good with the bad. We learn to embrace it all and use our strengths to carry us through the darker days. I did my best to embrace it all—even the dark times—because I knew they would get better.

And get better they did, as I stood in my kitchen with the two-lined plastic test stick all lit up with pink. I videotaped Brett finding out. I called my sister, crying. I lay in bed that night dreaming of how we would announce the news to friends and family. This isn't the kind of announcement to just "say." It needed to be *unveiled*. So I tediously painted "Soon-to-Be Big Sister" on a tiny T-shirt for Lainey and revealed a photo of her wearing it in an e-mail to friends. We wrote Brett's dad a birthday card telling him his present would be placed in his arms in November. Late November. I had always wanted a holiday baby, and this promised to be just as dreamy as I imagined.

Even after the first ultrasound when we were told, "It's okay . . . you're just not measuring as far as you think you are . . . but there's the little bean right there," Brett assured me everything was just fine. And so did everyone else. I was tired, and I loved being tired. Coffee made me queasy, and I loved that coffee made me queasy. But somewhere deep inside, I knew something was off.

On Sunday, March 29, we lost our hoped-for, dreamed-for, longed-for pregnancy. I knew early that weekend it was going to happen, yet the news was no less painful. I cried when I told Brett it was over. Heaved my body into full-fledged sobs on my bed as he hugged me and told me it was going to be okay. Pulled my knees to my chest with every cramp that reminded me the baby I wanted was leaving my body for good. Wiped my tears with a baby blanket I kept on my nightstand, a blanket that promised to hold what I yearned for. I cried and yet, at the same time, I felt strengthened by the fact that I was not the only one this had happened to . . . and this was very doable and surmountable compared to many other challenges in life. I felt strengthened by the fact that it happened early, and I did not have to feel kicks and leaps and lose not only the dream of that baby but the unspeakable bond heightened by feeling movement within me.

And in the end, I was proud of myself. Because I was not devastated. I was sad, yes. But I was happy for what I already had, and the promising future of more babies. I even found myself dancing in my living room to Madonna two days after I miscarried. Yes, dancing. Dancing like a crazy woman with my daughter, throwing my body to the rhythms of its splendor, its amazingness, its strength, feeling my girl's arms around my neck, her soft hair tickling my face as I tipped her back, forward, rocking to the beat . . . and laughing until tears rolled down my cheeks. And it felt so good.

This is what women do. We have complex bodies that create beings from microscopic cells, and when everything isn't *just right*, our bodies take over and do what they know to do. I marveled at the strength of my body. That it had the biological awareness to know that little bean wasn't poised to grow properly, and that it had the clockwork capabilities to take care of it—to heal itself and become better again.

But there was a different, darker side to my amazement as well. My body and my heart were separate entities—the former had betrayed the latter. And yes, it sucked. It sucked standing in line at the grocery store

holding a Stayfree bag when a month earlier I was in that same line holding the box of pregnancy tests that would turn all pink and make me cry.
It sucked going into Lainey's second-year scrapbook and erasing all that
stuff I wrote about her being a big sister that November. Or folding up
her big-sister shirt and hoping it would still fit when she could wear it
again. It sucked to lose what felt like half my body weight in blood or to
have to leave Baby Gap, embarrassingly pulling my shirt down behind
me because I was stupid enough to wear white jeans while I was having a
miscarriage. It sucked, but it was real.

And I think I finally understood. Understood that there is something to be said for the instinctive need to love a *little*. To want one in
your arms so bad it hurts. To understand that whether you want just one
or just one more, it hurts not to get it.

That weekend, I felt it deep in my soul—that instinctual love that already existed, that has existed since the beginning of time, for the next
child I wanted to hold. I loved her at that moment.

Two months later I was pregnant again. Everyone told me after my
miscarriage I'd be pregnant again soon, and whether they said it believing it or just to make me feel better, thank God they were right. I
invested every ounce of hope I had in those words.

Shortly after Lainey's two-year ladybug birthday bash, I peed on the
ever-present stick after doing the same thing just days earlier to get a
blank one, but this time? This time I got two pink lines. My heart did a
quiet leap, but I told it to settle down *just in case*. Seconds later, I scooped
up Lainey and booked it to the nearest drugstore to buy another box of
tests *just in case*. False hope is like being told you're going to Disney World
when you're eight years old only to arrive, days after holding your breath
with anticipation, to find a field of nothing, and being laughed at when
you cry. I didn't want to feel that barren landscape of disappointment,
and I knew those foolproof digital sticks would kill any doubt: *Pregnancy
Sticks for Dummies,* they were—no lines, no faint colors, no ambiguous
plus signs—just a clear "Pregnant" or "Not Pregnant" on a digital screen
and Lord, how I danced when I saw it . . . an indisputable "Pregnant."

I let my heart leap a little more wildly, a little more freely—even allowed it an awkward cartwheel or two, but it wasn't until a few weeks later when I heard the *whoosh-whoosh* of her beating heart, of life inside me, of the soul that would slowly dig its roots deep into mine where they belong and stay forever; it wasn't until that moment, lying under the thin scratchy paper of the exam table, that I let it happen. I accepted it. I smiled and cried and called my friends and family. And I let my heart dance its ass off. The sweet dance of beautiful, perfect life.

That afternoon, we celebrated. I joined friends at the local pub and while they drank, I passed around my ultrasound photos. I purposely wore a dress that made me look pregnant, and I rested my hand over my stomach—over my little bean—as green cotton cascaded loosely over my waist. I realized later this dress was entirely too short when I bent over to pick up Lainey's crayon and flashed my underwear to the bar behind me, but I didn't care. I was pregnant.

This bliss continued through the following weeks until one night when Brett was away on business. He had taken a new job that year working as a regional sales manager for a communications software company headquartered near Chicago, and it had recently demanded some challenging travel situations. I hated it. I hated being alone and pregnant, I hated knowing that Lainey missed him like crazy, and I hated that Brett was doing the best he could to be a responsible provider in this economy when really, his heart just yearned to be home with his family. And here I was, thirteen weeks pregnant, and I woke up in the middle of the night, alone with my girl, to wet sheets. My pajamas were soaked. After a bit of confusion and telling myself that thirty-year-olds don't exactly wet their beds, I got up and headed to the bathroom, only to find blood. Blood on me, on the sheets, all over the floor. And my mind immediately flashed back to the day our last pregnancy ended. In the dim glow of the night-light, I fell to the floor and cried. Begged God not to let this be happening. I fumbled for my phone and shook as I dialed as many numbers as I could. I couldn't get a hold of Brett. Or my sister. Or anyone I randomly dialed afterward. Why the hell won't anyone answer their phone in the middle of the night? Finally, my friend Carie calmly answered and assured me she'd be there to take me to the hospital.

We brought Lainey with us, all snuggled in her jammies. We were met in the emergency room by my friend Laura, who rocked Lainey in her arms for almost four hours in an uncomfortable waiting-room chair while Carie and I stayed in a tiny room behind a light blue curtain, clinging to what little hope I could manage to hold on to. Tears streamed down my cheeks for hours while we waited for the ultrasound. I couldn't control them, and even when I laughed at Carie's attempts to keep me happy by telling me embarrassing things that happened to her, I was fully aware that we were here because I was bleeding profusely—and I was thirteen weeks pregnant.

At 4:30 A.M., an ultrasound tech arrived to wheel my bed down long, empty corridors to a dark room where he closed the door and put warm jelly on my stomach. The stream of tears still flowed steadily as he typed numbers and clicked measurements onto the screen. He knew I was scared and yet, because of his training, I'm sure, he kept the mood light and distracting, telling me stories about his dogs, his mom who lived with him, how he moved here from Chicago.

"I love Chicago. It's my favorite city," I mumbled, attempting to connect with anything other than the gripping fear that I was about to be devastated. Again.

He turned the screen so I couldn't see.

"Can you just tell me if there's a heartbeat? Can you please tell me if the baby's okay?" I asked, choking back sobs.

"I'm sorry. I can't tell you anything. You'll have to wait for the doctor to read the ultrasound."

Silence and fear enveloped the room, and the only sound came from my tears. I wished the lights were on and the four walls of the small room weren't closing in on me. In the dark, the ultrasound tech from Chicago, the one whose mother lived with him, glided the wand across my stomach with a stoic face. Until he stopped for a moment and said. . .

"I'm not supposed to tell you anything, but . . ." and then he turned the screen my way and smiled.

He didn't have to say a word. There, on the screen, was a baby. A baby who moved and danced, and there—right there in the middle—was an unmistakable little beating heart. And that—*that was a beautiful moment.*

Released with instructions to stay in bed for a week and see my doctor the next day to find out what was going on, I returned home in the morning to be pampered and embraced by one of the biggest outpourings of love I had ever experienced. Brett was on his way home from Chicago the next day, but in the meantime my house was filled—at 6:30 in the morning—with jammy-wearing friends who hugged me and held me and screamed, "Get your ass back in bed!" in unison every time I even suggested I was going to stand up for a moment.

These women—my friends—stayed by my side, took care of my *little,* found out my favorite vegetable beef soup recipe, went to the store and came home with bags of ingredients that they chopped and simmered in my kitchen while they laughed and sipped wine, told stories, and reminded me of the joy that follows sadness. They brought lunch and smoothies and piles of movies. They cleaned my kitchen and folded my laundry, changed my sheets and scrubbed my bathroom. They had me in fits of laughter while I lay on my bed watching them organize piles of embarrassing clutter in my closet against my will.

I had been lying on the couch in my living room for no more than an hour that morning when my friend Wylie arrived. Wylie is funny and loud and unfiltered, the life of the party and definitely the one you want around when you are craving normalcy. Her sensitivity that morning surprised and touched me. She sat on my coffee table and leaned in, intently, genuinely, and whispered, "So I know what happened, but tell me again," and as I retold the day's events from the puddles of blood to that very moment, her eyes pooled with tears. She hurt for me—and I felt it. Then, calmly and beautifully, she continued, "I'm so sorry you had to go through that—but, babe, you stink. Get some goddamn deodorant." And our tears magically turned into heaves of rehabilitating laughter.

It felt like Christmas, being surrounded with the sounds of a lively kitchen, happy kids, small-talking girlfriends, and feeling the love of a village . . . *my village*. I don't think my friends really know what a force of love and strength they were for me that year—how they put the pieces of me back together. Women are amazing that way. I think we are good at seeing others in pain and internalizing it—recognizing what it would take for us to move on, what we would need to be healed, what we would hope someone would do to comfort us in that scenario—and then we do it for that person. And in my home that day, among the throng of women who came to patch up what was damaged, there was a small taste of what was to come.

It turned out that all that blood and all that panic came from a very big blood clot. A blood clot that kept me in bed for a week and had me in a fretful state of mind and mood but turned out to be harmless. They don't always end up that way though. Sometimes they induce labor.

Sometimes the baby doesn't make it. But our baby? She was strong. She knew we needed her—and she made it.

I've been saying "she" like I knew all along, but the morning of my gender ultrasound, I was in knots. I know it's honorable and everything to say you just want a healthy baby, but I'd be lying if I said I didn't want another girl—and so did Brett. I am learning the older I get to stop pretending I think something just because it's right. Real is sometimes better than right, and what's real is that I wanted another girl so bad I didn't even pick out a boy's name. I carried a tiny pink sock around from the day I found out I was pregnant—literally safety-pinned it to my purse—and the morning of the ultrasound, I rubbed its nubby threads between my fingers as if it were some sort of silly superstitious ritual that would actually reverse a penis if there was one.

"So what do you think?" Brett asked. He poured me a glass of orange juice and handed it to me with my vitamins as I scurried around the kitchen, running late as usual.

"I think it's a girl." I stumbled over the words, careful to disconnect myself enough to build a small protective barrier just in case. I wanted Lainey to have a sister. She was already twice blessed with incredible brothers and, having a sacred sister bond myself, I wanted that for her. I wanted to say "my girls," reuse bonnets and tights, read *Little Women* to two bodies snuggled under rosebud sheets, overhear gossip about boys, and break up fights over clothes and curling irons.

"You think we'll get lucky? Can you imagine—two girls to go with my two boys? I mean, seriously. How good can we get it?" Brett smiled, and I knew he too was being cautious to hope for something so silly—so shallow. "It doesn't matter," he added. "We'll be blessed either way." And with that, he kissed me, walked our girl out to her car seat, buckled her in, and waved good-bye.

An hour later, I held my breath with my firstborn by my side, snuggled up next to me on the ultrasound table just like she always did, and we watched together as Dr. Jody squinted her eyes and looked intently into the screen.

"See that right there?" She pointed to a spot and went on, "That's a girl." Clouds parted, angels sang, heaven opened its doors, and I think I saw my grandma wave.

The rest of the pregnancy went perfectly. Nella Cordelia was on her way, and we couldn't wait for her arrival. Every ultrasound showed a beautiful baby girl—a couple of them even had her high-kickin', which led to comments like "She's going to be a dancer!" or "Just wait till she kicks that soccer ball." I even opted out of the triple-marker blood test at the halfway point because I knew things were great and didn't want any false negatives draining any of the joy I was feeling. I had my family and my home and these phenomenal mommy days of painting and

picnics and baking cookies with Lainey. All the while I yearned for the coming joy of a new *little* bursting into our idyllic lives, making everything even more beautiful. I felt so completely blessed. Because life is messy and my life had certainly had its pains, but the fact that the overall plan for my adult life seemed to be panning out smoothly was so incredibly comforting. Not that we didn't have our bumps. Brett's job was requiring a lot of travel and his being away from home had definitely added its stress on our family, but I knew things could only get better. In fact, before Christmas, after a particularly stressful week of Brett's, being gone and coming home exhausted and missing us, I remember telling him, "It will all be better soon, babe. It can only get better from here."

December was my last month with my only daughter. I drank the last sips of that cup gratefully and purposefully, cherishing the splendor of everything she had been to me for the past years and making note of how wonderful it felt to really be with her, without distraction, every time we set out in the afternoon on our walks—me with my big round belly, and her with her wayward pigtails and scuffed-up sneakers. I couldn't imagine motherhood getting any sweeter than it already tasted, and yet I knew from all the stories of my friends who had welcomed new babies into their families and went through that whole heart-stretching-even-more thing that it would indeed be more beautiful. I was going to give Lainey a sister. I was going to give her a best friend. Someday they would know each other's thoughts from just a look, and one day, they would have each other on speed dial to complain about kids mouthing off and husbands who don't pick up after themselves.

And, in the last weeks before January 22, 2010, I felt overwhelmed with excitement. I felt like the next chapters of our lives were going to be amazing. In fact, right before the new year, before Nella's birth, on the eve of my thirty-first birthday, I wrote the following words:

It's taken me awhile to grasp it all, but I have finally arrived at the grown-up place of life-is-what-you-make-it and there are lots of things in life we go through that aren't comfortable or ideal, but they could be so incredibly worse, and a simple life of comfort does nothing to change us, mold us, make us into better, stronger more beautiful versions of ourselves. . .

I have been reminded so much these past couple weeks of just how wonderfully blessed we are, and the older I get, the more I embrace change as an opportunity to learn just what I am capable of.

I am capable of so much.

. . . and I am excited at the opportunity of new challenges, more love . . . Perhaps I had been planted for too long and this little bit of discomfort will challenge me, in my thirty-first year, to push myself more toward new chapters in the story of our life.

They will be good chapters.

The last few days have been such a snowballing of emotions and contemplations and yes, hormones, to settle me into a contented place of so-be-it. Life flows on, and I want to experience every tide, every wave, every calm with purpose.

And I think somewhere inside, something was preparing me. To ready my heart for what was about to come. Somewhere inside, *I knew.*

chapter 2
h o m e

PEOPLE OFTEN ASK ME HOW I FOUND THE STRENGTH to see the glass as half full when I brought our Nella home to begin the next chapter in our story. First, let me tell you something about strength. You can't buy it, and you most certainly cannot get it overnight. It is earned, like muscle sinews that grow and fortify over years of hard exercise. Second, I wouldn't say my glass is always half full. There are days when it's cracked and leaking, days when it's chipped and even shattered. But then I get the Krazy Glue out and fix it, and suddenly it's half full again. Even though it's patched up in places, I've made it my own with the beveled edges and beautiful etchings that perspective brings.

And don't think for a second that my view of the ideal family has always been the whole white-picket-fence fantasy. My fence may have started out white, but it wasn't long before I realized that color can be fabulous and that the houses that truly stand out may be fenced with fuchsia or turquoise or a good crazy yellow. My fence is loud and vibrant, and I am proud of the many shades it's been painted, but somewhere, way back when, it was indeed white.

My most foundational childhood memories began on Horseshoe Drive—in a trilevel home with brown shutters and a well-kept lawn. They are the happiest of my young memories, and I owe it all to my parents. While neither of them are or have ever been perfect, they approached making meaningful childhood memories for us like it was an Olympic sport, finishing not gold—no, that would be too flashy, too storybook, too staged—but maybe silver or bronze, an even more honorable achievement: just as much effort with less glory.

I am the baby of the family. My brother, Bubby (whose given name is Christopher, but that's about as meaningful as knowing a banana's scientific name), is the oldest, and he was brave, and a genius to boot, spending much of our childhood rigging up dangerous stunts to put on shows for our cousins. He once built a zip line in our backyard that went between two large trees and threatened paralysis, but we all, thankfully, conquered it unscathed. Carin, my older sister, was shy and fragile. When she cried, my brother would say, "Fragile's crying again," which would, in turn, make Fragile cry even harder. Carin and I shared a room in our brown-shuttered house. It had purple shag carpet that no one ever saw because it was always hidden by a shitload of stuff that covered the floor. This mess would build for several months until my dad would finally banish us to our room and tell us we couldn't come out until it

was clean. And we'd sit there for hours—lying on top of our clothes and books, trying to get motivated to clean—until we realized he was actually serious and we really wouldn't see the light of day until we crammed everything into our closet and under the bed. We even made up games to motivate each other. My sister would pick up the phone (which was a plastic frog that *ribbited* when it rang) and pretend it was the president of the United States.

"Uh-huh . . . uh-huh. Okay, Mr. President. We'll see you in an hour." And then she'd hang up and jump up and down screaming that the president was coming and we had to get our room clean. We knew damn well that frog phone had nothing but a dial tone on the other end and that the president would not be pulling up to Horseshoe Drive in an hour, but for some reason, this sham worked for both of us. We'd fly—like *crazy fly*—around our room, throwing things in drawers, cramming stuff in closets, all the while frantically screaming to each other, "Five more minutes! Five more minutes!" If the scars I sported from all the times my sister scratched me with her Lee Press-On nails didn't bond us, then sharing a room and having to frantically clean before the president's arrival certainly did.

We were PKs—Pastor's Kids. My dad pastored the North Metro Free Methodist Church in Troy, Michigan, a few miles away from our house, and we fit, or so everyone thought, the traditional mold for a pastor's perfect family. We went to church every Sunday and learned about Noah and Jonah and Daniel and the lion's den through flannelgraph Bible lessons and Popsicle stick crafts. On Wednesday nights, my mom would bake brownies for the couples' group that would meet downstairs in our family room, and my sister and I would lurk around the kitchen, stealing food from the dishes they brought. We entertained a lot of families, and I have many good memories of pot roast in the Crock-Pot and Steve

Green cassette tapes accompanying the hubbub of my mom and dad cleaning house, lighting candles, and getting ready to host friends. "Rik & Kris," my parents, were a sort of Christian representation of Ken & Barbie, and we little "Skippers" followed suit, fulfilling the polished image of a pastor's family as best we could.

Every Christmas Eve, my dad held a candlelight service at the church. We'd arrive, wearing red sweaters and new tights, and I'd be sporting two braids that my mom perfectly wove with my fine brown hair. Bubby would make Carin cry in the car and Carin would, in turn, take it out on me so that when we got to the church, we were all upset and crying. But then, like magic—at least in my mind—things turned to perfection. My dad would preach while we were allowed to sit out on the front step of the church, looking toward the sky because we didn't want to miss a glimpse of Santa. And for the rest of the night and the following day, we lived the storybook family life I remember so fondly during those years.

I'm glad I have those memories, because they didn't last forever. From what I can remember though, every Christmas, the planets aligned, the stars were just a little bit brighter, and in a little house on Horseshoe Drive, we were the perfect family with a white picket fence. My mom baked a cinnamon St. Lucia crown for Christmas breakfast every year, complete with tiny poinsettia petals made from red maraschino cherries and little leaves from the green ones. We awoke, in our new pajamas, to a wonderland of magic my parents stayed up all night creating—strings leading to thoughtful gifts, music humming, scents wafting, and smiles—always smiles. We huddled on the floor to hear the story of the Nativity before we opened presents, and we gathered new toys in bags later in the day to take with us on our trip to my grandparents' house for more merriment. It was a grand representation of the kinds of things my parents did all year long to create a memorable childhood. School projects, birthday parties, classroom baked goods, vacations, sewing projects, holidays—it never ended. They made life "big" for us, and we learned, early on, that pouring yourself into activities to make life special for your kids is worth all the sweat and tears and helps chisel grooves into personalities that will later find beauty in "living big" too.

While I may have forgotten a lot of my painful memories, I will never forget the day Pastor Ken and Mrs. Barbie and all the little Skippers got their parsonage rocked. It was November 3, 1987. It was a Tuesday, and I was most likely gazing at Scott Bannerton in my third-grade class when my name was called over the PA system and the voice coming through the speaker told me to go to the office with all my belongings so I could go home early. In third grade, that was like the coolest thing that could ever happen to you outside of winning at four-square or completing a perfect round-off on the blacktop at recess with merited applause. I walked down the hallway, dragging my backpack behind me, wondering what cool, spontaneous thing my parents were up to. A surprise trip perhaps or maybe shopping, just me and my dad? Instead, I was met in the office by my mom, a little solemn faced, who told me my brother and sister were waiting in the car for me. And they were—along with my grandma and bags of all our clothes. Once the car got moving, we were told we were going away to my cousin's house. And we would never come back.

It was an hour-and-a-half drive to my cousin's. And in trauma time, that's like six hours. So, for what seemed like six hours, my mom and grandma did what you do when you love your littles and want to spare them from hurt. You pretend it's okay. You fake smile and tell stories and overcompensate for the slightest moment of awkward silence with forced normalcy. You point out stupid billboards on the side of the road and talk about all the fun you're going to have when you arrive because you're not only attempting to comfort your children, you're trying to convince yourself at the same time that everything's going to be okay. And I half believed them and their bullshit stories of this-is-going-to-be-fun. I half convinced myself that the false net of security my mom was trying to create was real and that the heaping bags of all my stuff in the backseat were just a figment of my imagination. And I only half paid attention to that aching ball of pain that was creeping up my throat, welling up in my eyes for what I thought this just might be . . . my parents' divorce. I don't remember a lot, but I do remember crying—not for me, but for my mom and dad. I didn't want either one of them to be sad, and I didn't want either one of them to feel like we chose the other parent.

Divorce sucks. And then there are some divorces that *really* suck. My parents' was the latter. There are things I didn't know that November Friday. Things I wouldn't find out for a while and things my mom and dad had been going through for a very long time. But somewhere in between climbing into the van with my clothes packed up in bags and settling into a new town where we moved in with some friends of my aunt's, I was told why our family was falling apart.

I wish I could remember it—the moment I was told. I wish I could conjure up the emotions that I so easily associate with my babies' births—the details of what I was doing and where my little eight-year-old self

was standing and what she was thinking when it all came to be. But I can't. I don't remember who told me or where I was or what I felt, but somewhere, somehow, someone told me that we would never be a family again. Somewhere, somehow, someone told me that *my dad was gay.*

At this point, it would make sense to say I cried. It would make sense to say I was embarrassed or ashamed or confused—that I lay on my bed and curled up in a fetal position and didn't get up until morning. But I didn't. I was eight. I actually don't think I even knew what gay was then, but the beauty of this is that I'd like to think if I was told that news again today, I would react much like I did those many years ago. I was sad—yes. But I was sad because I knew my mom was sad. And I was sad because I knew my dad was sitting in our house by himself missing us. I pictured him opening drawers in our bedroom, seeing the clothes we left and crying. It wasn't until I chanted a song I made up, "Hey, hey, my dad is gay," and got quickly hushed that I realized gay was different—something a lot of people had a problem with.

My mom was hurt. And it's hard to understand what that would be like. She found solace in her faith and, soon, in the church that embraced a single mom and her three kids who left the gay pastor dad; but, while church can be a beautiful place where souls are fed and hearts are healed, it can also be a place of judgment, false representations of God, and a place by which people define themselves against others. There is a big difference between Church and God, and over the next several years Church took over, slowly painting over my view of God with big scary brushstrokes and dark, intimidating colors.

"Your dad is going to hell," Church told me. And then Church said I would too if I accepted him. "If you really love your dad," Church went on, "you will separate from him and show him that he cannot live like this." I was very scared of Church. And I certainly didn't want to go to hell. So I told my dad I didn't want to be with him when I was eight years old. I said it while knots in my stomach twisted and turned and begged me to accept him, to run into his arms and tell him I wanted to live on Horseshoe Drive again with all of us and be a happy family.

A nasty custody battle ensued. For over a year, we were dragged to counseling, sat in friend-of-the-court meetings, and packed our bags for weekend visitation, all the while still listening to Church and watching as the kind and loving God we once knew slowly disappeared under layers of dark, scary colors. Looking back, the battle wasn't so much between my mom and dad. They were both good, loving parents who wanted the best for us. We were all just pawns in a bigger battle of Church versus Gay, an eternal struggle all over the world that's still going on today.

Church won for years. While my dad was rebuilding his life with a new job as a hospital chaplain and with a new man who would someday, years later, stand in a hospital room holding my daughter with tears streaming down his face after we were told she was "different," we slowly grew apart. I learned to hide the fact that the dad I never saw was gay, to blush when my friends threw the word around like it was bad, to pray that God would "turn him around," and to beg that, regardless, he would never ever send my dad to hell.

What I lacked in a fatherly role model and gained in a crumbling depiction of God during those years, my mother made up for in her consistent love for us. She may have been hurting, confused, and distracted with Church, but she never lost her way in how she loved us. My mom is quiet and steady, a constant presence in my life, and when the waters of her life have ever turned to swirling rapids, she has swum with the current without complaining. She laughs when she swims and makes fun of herself and the way her arms flail when she's trying to stay afloat. She grips rocks to keep from drowning, and while she's holding on for dear life, she's giggling about how funny she looks while doing it. Humor. She has it, and she has shown me that sometimes, the funniest moments come when we are barely hanging on.

When I was sixteen and thoroughly screwed up from Church, I began to wonder if perhaps there was something bigger out there. I wondered if maybe I had it all wrong and if there was more to God and to life than just fearfully walking the tightrope of don't-screw-up-or-you'll-burn-in-hell. I wanted my dad back in my life, and I wanted to figure things out for myself. So I called him one day, without anyone knowing. I called my dad and told him I wanted to see him. It was awkward and forced and I didn't know what to say, but I knew I was taking a step toward where I wanted to go . . . toward where I wanted to end up.

One visit led to another and another, and soon I was spending weekends at his house and going to the movies with him and his friend, Gary. It was strange how normal it felt—like there was no time lost. I had a room in their house. After all those lost years, I had a room that was mine. A room and a dad, and I knew we both felt it—that the emptiness that had existed had finally been filled. I was overjoyed to have a dad again and comforted by the fact that my mom was growing more secure with it all, with herself and her future, and soon, my brother and sister followed suit. I think we all knew there was more to life than the confined restrictions by which we had been living, and at the same time, we were all setting out on a journey to discover for ourselves what it was all about . . . our purpose, our happiness, our life. Little did we know that someday we'd all celebrate Christmas together again.

I finally saw my dad as just Dad and not as a gay man anymore. I saw him as a great father who, like every other father, had strengths and weaknesses and just wanted to be happy. It took a long time to repaint our fence again, to peel through the layers of pain and arrive to where we are today. We are a unique family. We are imperfect, and we let fear shape us for too long. We have a painful past painted all shades of ugly, but our present is beautiful. We can all come together now and celebrate births and birthdays and Christmas Eves. We have regained control of our game pieces and are no longer pawns but active players in the game of life, together.

As for Church? I don't think Church means harm. I think there are people who find hope in Church—amazing people who love and give and work hard to bring good to the world—and perhaps don't understand that there is something bigger, something better, something that cannot be confined to four walls and a steeple or to a book or a sermon or a pastor. People seek comfort in rules and find security in establishments, but through every pain and joy in my life, I have drawn closer to the grander amazement that God is big and accessible and, like any parent who loves a child, he wants us to find joy and good in life. I have found that joy and good are everywhere—in many people from all walks of life and belief systems, and that while I believe in God and feel his presence in the events in my life, I feel him as love rather than fear or judgment. I am certain that forgiveness and reconciliation beget good and can only draw one closer to the mystery and wonder that is God.

When my dad accepted the job as hospital chaplain, I think he found himself in his work. While Church is a great establishment that serves its purpose for many people, sometimes it can fall short and miss the big picture. Sometimes it fails to see that love and kindness and acceptance should trump rules and principles, a board of directors, and books with a section A, part 2, line 4 that says things like *Church membership shall not be granted to anyone who . . .* In a hospital, you have to understand all faiths or even the lack of faith. Illness and surgery and birth and death are common passages for the entire human family, regardless of beliefs, and the fact that they happen to everyone unifies us. This all-

embracing line of work unlocked in my dad an amazing ability to help others through joy and pain.

I've seen my dad at work. I've been with him when he walks into a hospital room and holds the hand of the dying. When he welcomes babies joyously and says prayers with new parents, initiating the celebration of life. When he's discovered a cancer patient who doesn't have much time has always wanted to go to Hawaii, so he secretly plans with nurses for days to throw a luau on her unit, instructing caretakers to wear leis, piping Don Ho music into her hospital room, taping palm tree pictures to the wall, and watching as her family tearfully smiles and gratefully offers their thanks. He welcomes and embraces all religions and races and belief systems and sees not the differences of the faces that walk into his hospital but the similarities in their hearts. Because we all suffer through losses and we all rejoice when good things happen. And that acceptance and celebration of life and the little things? *That* is God.

When Nella was born and we were told she had Down syndrome, it wasn't but a minute when I said, "I want my dad." And I can't imagine if I would have let those years of pain and judgment keep me from knowing who he is today. I can't imagine lying in that hospital bed with the weight of a dismal future on my shoulders and not seeing my dad's smile, his teary eyes, his arms outstretched to take my girl, or hearing him say, "That's okay. We love her." My friends say later that night—after she was born—that he was whistling in the hallway. He whistled while I cried and the echo of that whistle resonated through the hallway to my friends who were huddled on the floor in tears. He helped initiate a wave of healing and acceptance when, throughout his own life, he had been faced with the opposite. He told me my girl was perfect when the world told me otherwise.

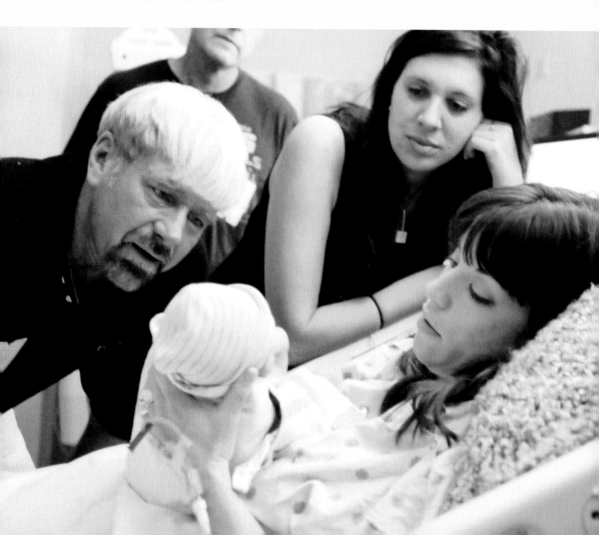

A few weeks after her birth, I asked my dad to write his own account of what he remembered that day. He had shared many moments with others in the hallway outside my room—moments I wanted to know about, to carve the grooves of change and growth in my heart even deeper, and I knew his perspective would help me in my journey. In his account, he recalled walking into my room to be told the news that had just changed my world forever:

> My daughter's voice, as she began the six words that would forever change our lives, was apologetic . . . almost an appeal. An appeal to accept, to love, to receive. "They think she has Down syndrome," she said—no softening preface, no commentary after . . . just fading down to the smile still sending its plea to accept the news and the sweet one she was snuggling close. While something within me wanted to cry to the heavens, "No," a softer yet stronger voice simply said, "Well, we love her . . . she's our gift." Other words were spoken, I am sure, but I don't remember them. I was reordering myself—walking around in my mind, looking for doors to be opened, finding them only in my heart. I just wanted to hold my baby and have everyone else go away. I wanted to begin to feel what this was and where we were going. And then I heard my daughter's voice again, as she lifted Nella toward me, asking, "Can you pray?" And my throat suddenly burned as my arms moved without thought to cradle this little one who fit so beautifully in them. And I suddenly just wanted to thank God for her . . . for all of her . . . for what we knew and what we didn't know. And I wonder if gratitude is the uniformed doorman of the heart needing to be healed. I do know tears must improve vision, for Nella looked even more beautiful through my weeping eyes.

When I first read that part of his account, I had my own experience with improved vision through weeping eyes. For it dawned on me exactly what those words meant: *We love her . . . she's our gift.* Such little words that represent a grander, greater lesson of acceptance and love—a lesson I had been faced with so many other times in my life and failed at, and now my dad was teaching me how to open my heart and love. My picket fence was being painted once again—a vibrant and rich hue. Far from a flawless white, but because of that, even more beautiful.

And what is it about perfection that makes it so appealing? The white picket fence, the polished image of Ken & Barbie and their perfect Skippers who are pretty and smart and heterosexual? What is it about *different* that makes us think it's not perfect? We set the bar higher and higher, and what is it we strive for, and once we reach it—this perfection—what have we achieved? It's never enough.

Through pain and growth, I have come to appreciate—no, more than that—I've come to *love* my fence, even though it may be different from the neighbors'. The concept of *perfection* is not flawless or ripped from a magazine. It's happiness. Happiness with all its messiness and *not-quite-thereness*. It's knowing that life is short, and the moments we choose to fill our cup with should be purposeful and rich. That we should be present for life, that we should drink deeply. And *that's* perfection. And my dad and my mom and my family—my past, present, and future with our Nella, what the world may view as broken or damaged—have taught me what true beauty really is.

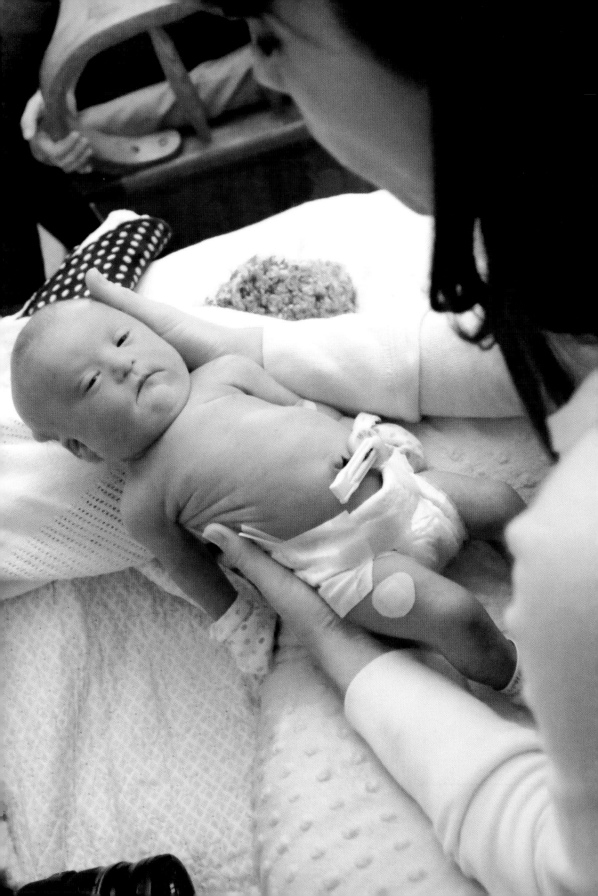

chapter 3

room 16

HEALING IS A BIT LIKE WATCHING A FLOWER BLOOM.
You don't really know when it's going to happen, and despite the
fact that you might be sitting there in front of barren ground attempting to will a bare stem to blossom, it doesn't happen on
command. No, it is gradual. Like time-lapse photography. And
as you are sitting, waiting, pleading for growth, you eventually
begin to forget that you are waiting until suddenly, days later, you
look and behold . . . *a bloom*.

Although I might not have known it, my heart began its healing process the moment my eyes met Nella's for the first time.
It was painful. And brutal. And would be followed by moments
that seem so far from bloom-worthy, you'd think my little seed
had been dug up and abandoned. But, no. Healing was there,
burrowing its roots deep into my heart, painfully yet purposefully cutting through, the way the strong roots do until they are
grounded deep enough to anchor what they know will follow—
growth.

I woke up on January 23, the day after Nella was born, to a dark hospital room. And when I say I "woke up," I mean I decided to get out of bed for the day because I never slept that night. I closed my eyes to numb the pain a bit, but never slept. It was 5:45 A.M., Katie was asleep next to me in bed, her arm wrapped around my waist where Nella was snuggled in a nook between us, and Heidi was half asleep on the pull-out couch next to the bed, her semireclining position suggesting she was attentive and willing to jump up and help when she heard the slightest of my cries. I recalled for a moment what I thought this morning would be. How I had imagined it a week before. That sunlight would be streaming into the windows of my happy, flower-strewn room and I would be nursing my baby, victoriously smiling, awaiting the throng of visitors. And here I was, beaten down, despairing, drowning in the darkness of a room that held so much sadness. I looked down at the tiny bundle nestled next to me and traced her lips with my finger. Her perfect little lips. I watched her chest rise and fall peacefully next to me as I slipped out of bed, snuggling her next to Katie so she wouldn't be alone. I wanted Brett. I wanted the room to fill with friends. I wanted to see sunshine and to shed the sadness so badly. So I took the first step to newness I could think of—a shower.

I'll never forget that shower. I'll never forget shedding my nightgown in that tiny bathroom and looking down to see the absence of her—my stomach was gone. And the sadness gripped me. Suffocated me. I wanted that stomach back so badly, wanted to have some reminder of the happiness I had—of the perfect baby I imagined was burrowed inside me. It was over. There was no beautiful bulge that kicked and pressed her feet against me. Just the doughy remains of what was. I was cold and couldn't manage to get the water warm enough from the measly trickle that dripped out of the hospital showerhead. I didn't want to wake Heidi or Katie after what I had put them through that night, but I couldn't take it anymore. I pressed my hand against the cold tile in front of me, leaned over, and let my body and my heart do what they needed to do—sob . . . hard.

"Heidi," I cried, hoping she might be able to hear me over the water stream. "Heidi!" I called again, desperate for company. And then she appeared, and I lost it. "I can't be in here alone. I can't do this. I can't breathe." I stood there cold, naked, and literally gasping for air.

"I'm right here," she affirmed, and I watched as my friend dragged a rocking chair into that tiny bathroom, right next to the shower, and plopped her exhausted body into it. "I'll keep talking," she said, and I listened to her as I lathered my hair, shaved my legs, and tried to will the trickling lukewarm water to wash away my heartache.

"THE NET," MY FRIENDS CALL IT—THE EVER-PRESENT existence of one another, standing by, ready to catch any one of us who might be falling. We've all needed it at different times over the years. My friend Kelly needed it when she went through four years of infertility and two in-vitros. We'd huddle up at a bar after one of her disappointing blood tests and tell her it was going to be all right. That she was going to be a mama someday. That her body was not broken and that periods, yes, indeed sucked. And we'd sit for hours, telling stories, crying, laughing, bonding over cold beers with lots of limes. And then there was the occasional bad day for any one of us. And a battle cry would disperse over text or e-mail or down the line of our trusty phone tree. We've been there for one another through getting married, having babies, stressing at work, arguing with husbands, loving family, you name it. We gather over brunch at our favorite coffee shops and cover one another's asses when we're late to pick up kids or forget to bring a birthday present. And the moment the battle cry went out just minutes after my girl arrived that January evening, they were there for me. In droves.

AS I STEPPED OUT OF THE SHOWER AND TOOK THE TOWEL Heidi held out for me, I knew they'd be here soon. I didn't have to ask. I knew there were secret schedules and quiet phone calls being made in the hallway, reporting my status, arranging the troops. Months later I would ask them each how they were told and what they felt, but I didn't know at the time. I didn't know a birthday party celebration came to a crashing halt the evening before when the phone call came in. I didn't know my friend Stephanie fell to her knees on the cement in Marsha's driveway and cried for me while others helped her up or that Rayna walked out of the hospital, got into her car, laid her head on her steering wheel, and shook with sobs. I didn't know she was angry with God. What I did know was that they'd be here, as long as I needed them, and they would be here soon.

Heidi walked out into the room, leaving me in the bathroom for just a moment while she searched for my bag, a hair dryer, and some makeup I had packed in a pretty pink case tied with a ribbon. She brought it back into the bathroom, plopped it on top of the toilet, and reclaimed her seat in the rocking chair crowding the tiny space. "Thank you," I whispered. I wanted to tell her more—to thank her for the support during the tormenting night before, to ask her if she missed her kids, to tell her she could go home if she wanted to . . . but I couldn't.

I looked in the mirror. It was horrifying. My face was pale and peaked and my eyes—oh, my eyes. I could barely see them. Tiny slits engulfed in puffy, red, thick skin that swallowed my existence. I didn't recognize myself. And then, I did something strange. I attempted humor.

"Oh, Heidi, *I* look like I have Down syndrome." It was terribly inappropriate and completely awkward to muster but, for some reason, it felt good. We looked at each other, scared to acknowledge what I had just done, and stood in silence for all of about three seconds before the laughter came. It was still forced a little on my end, but it soothed, like healing balm. I laughed. I laughed in the eye of the storm, after the most excruciating evening of my life. And if I could laugh now, maybe this would turn out okay.

I didn't feel like I had just had a baby. After Lainey, I was a mess "downstairs" for days after, popping Motrin and Percocet as often as they'd let me, and here I was just hours after pushing a baby out and I felt nothing. I wondered why. Was the emotional pain so bad that I didn't notice the physical pain? Or perhaps my physical body wisely suspected there was too much agony already and graciously bowed out of the competition. Either way, I wanted to feel it. I wanted to feel like a mom again and experience every aspect of the ceremonious act of giving birth every other mom got to feel, but I felt nothing. I bled—yes—swiftly losing all the internal components that were a part of that beautiful nine months of growth, but still . . . I felt nothing.

Heidi cheerfully accompanied me in that bathroom as I washed my face and painted on pink lips and flushed cheeks. *Fake it till you make it,* I told myself. And so I dried my hair, pruned my brows, and slipped a pretty necklace over my head. I tried to curl my lashes but my lids were so swollen I couldn't do it without pinching a hunk of skin, so I left them bare. I slipped into the soft cotton gray dress my friend Stephanie let me borrow for this very day. Comfortable and yet pretty. And I wore leg warmers, because the chill of sadness was every bit as physical as it was emotional. It felt strange unpacking that bag—the bag that I had carefully put together, selecting comfortable cottons, new mama pajamas, and lots of pink for my girl. And now, it felt like I was unpacking someone else's bag, digging through clothes that had been packed for a different occasion—a happier one.

Primping completed, I felt a bit more capable to deal with the day. And then I remembered she was still sleeping, and I wanted her. I wanted my new daughter. I wanted to hold her again against my new fresh self and nurse her because I knew she needed me, and I knew I needed to begin my process of knowing her. Of deeply loving her. Of slowly bandaging the hurts of the previous evening and all I had said. All I had thought.

Katie had to head back to Fort Lauderdale, but before she left she hugged me tight. "You're gonna be fine, Kel. I know you're sad, but you're gonna be fine soon. I'll call you later. She's precious and beautiful, and I'm so in love with her." She kissed my girl and smiled as she waved and walked out the door, but I knew she'd cry when she hit her car. She had been such a rock, so positive, so happy, so encouraging that night, surely

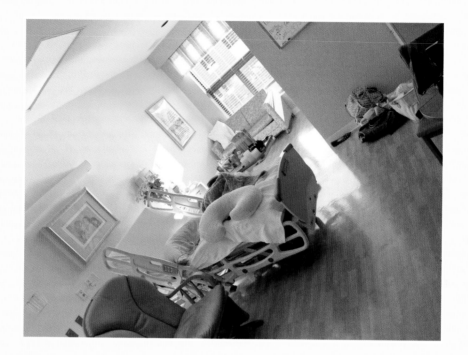

any of her sadness would finally be able to come to the surface and brew once she was on her way home, alone.

"All right, the girls are on their way and want to know what you want for breakfast," Heidi said as she hung up the phone and started cleaning the room. For the five days we eventually spent in that hospital room, Heidi must have cleaned it twenty times. I think it was her way of fixing what was broken. If she couldn't mend the sadness, couldn't allow me to see the hope that was to come, she could at least kick some ass in Room 16. There wasn't a moment without the glow of flameless candles, the scent of lavender oil, the movement of flower vases to different corners of the room, or little piles of stuff tidied into perfect order. Heidi feng-shuied her heart out, and while everything else felt like it was falling apart, the room was always, *always* perfectly together.

"I want a Dunkin' Donuts coffee with cream. That's it." My one pleasure. And I needed it.

"Kelle, you need to eat something." I knew Heidi was worried about me, but I also knew I couldn't eat. Just thinking about swallowing made me feel like I was drowning—like sadness had filled every hollow in my body and forcing food down would only stifle even more the little room I had left to breathe. And yet I knew Nella needed me. She needed me to eat because I was all she had. I wanted to take care of her, to feel like I was doing something good for her in the midst of my inabilities to rise to the occasion of being her mama like I wanted to—and eating something and transforming it to good, nourishing milk was the one thoughtless process I could do to help her.

"How 'bout a protein smoothie? I think I might be able to drink something and maybe they can get one of those good ones with all the fat and protein in it." It wasn't a matter of maybe. I knew any one of my friends would feel honored to do something for me—*anything* when they felt otherwise so helpless to alleviate my pain. Asking them to stop to bring me a smoothie would be a specific act of love they'd be happy to fulfill.

And within ten minutes they began to arrive. I sat in my hospital bed, my leg-warmer-hugged legs tucked beneath me while I held my sleeping girl, her body wrapped tightly in a blanket with her name on it and a hand-knit hat stretched tightly around her perfect head. Day One. We could do this. It wasn't going to be easy, but we'd get through it. The sun was just stretching its rays into our room, Brett would be here soon with Lainey, my dad was probably on his way, and somewhere, my sister was frantically packing her bags to board a plane to get here. We could do this. And, as my friends began to trickle in the room that morning for Aftershock Treatment, I slowly began to feel peace.

A quiet knock on the door signaled their arrival and I braced myself for each entrance, knowing some faces would set me off again, meeting their eyes, feeling their pain for me. As the first group of girls made their appearance, I'll never forget searching through the crowd for the one I needed to see. The one who knew my heartache. I needed to see her smile . . . *Marsha*.

Marsha is a strong and beautiful woman who smiles with her eyes. It's a genuine smile, but it's not without its scars. Marsha and I had our babies just weeks apart years earlier, my wispy-haired Lainey making it to my arms while her little Brady struggled to breathe in an isolette for weeks before he was able to go home. We helped Marsha love that boy for four beautiful months before we joined her to say good-bye. And although we were so fortunate to have our Nella healthy in our arms while sweet Brady didn't survive, I knew Marsha understood my pain, the pain of the unexpected. I knew she would hold my hand and look into my eyes and smile. I knew she would not apologize or pity me, but that she would tell me it was going to be all right. And if Marsha, after all she had been through, would tell me it was going to be all right, I would believe her. Though I cried when I met her eyes and felt the cosmic connection of *I've been there, babe*, with her warm glance, I was quickly comforted when she sat next to me, leaned over, and smiled with all her purity, "Oh, Kelle, she's beautiful." And I knew, Marsha says what Marsha means. Marsha thought she was beautiful. And I believed her.

Despite the fact that things were different than I had expected that day, I still had a baby. I still had her bag packed with beautiful things she would wear when the world would meet her and all the little hats I had anticipated would hug her sweet little head. I had a bottle of Burt's Bees buttermilk lotion that I couldn't wait to massage into her cheeks and smooth across her soft cowlick so that she would smell just like Lainey did the first day of her life. There were a whole lot of people who would hold my girl that day, and she was ready—smelling sweet and new, clothed in pink nubby cotton and wearing a homemade Valentine hat with a little stitched heart. I inhaled her cookie-sweet cheeks and smiled before I passed her to my friend Stephanie who, in true Stephanie fashion, stepped to the front of the line, holding out her arms and smiling, "I get her first."

While Stephanie cooed and slipped into her own little world with Nella in the corner, I looked around to see that the room was full. Marsha was curled up comfortably at the end of my hospital bed like we were sharing a beanbag in a college dormitory room; my friends Theresa, Rayna, and Samantha had found corners of couches and chairs to burrow into; Laura and Carie had just arrived with coffee and bagels; and Heidi, miraculously, after her call of duty in the night, was awake and lively, straightening piles and bags in the background. I had just talked to Brett who, strangely, sounded rested and happy and was anxious to bring Lainey back up to see us. And finally, my dad burst through the door smiling and embarrassingly singing "New York, New York" for all the nurses to hear.

"Start spreadin' the news . . ." He even threw in a little high kick for good measure and my girlfriends broke into peals of laughter.

"Dad, stop, you're embarrassing me."

"Where's our girl?" he asked, and he looked over to see her snuggled in Stephanie's arms and zoomed in to steal her away.

And then I stopped and drank it in. What was happening? It was nine o'clock in the morning, and while Room 16, just hours ago, felt like a torture chamber, it was slowly becoming a happy place. Hell, with my dad here, it was the freakin' Tony Awards. And I had the first of thousands of self-talks with myself. Encouraging self-talks that slowly and gently would transform the old version of me into the new version I would become.

They're happy, I told myself. *They're holding her and they're smiling and they're happy.* Maybe this wasn't the end of the world. Maybe, with everyone's help, I could do this and I could do it well.

But I still knew it would be a long day. I knew I'd be gripped with sadness again when Lainey came to play with her little sister, when social workers came in to dump piles of Down syndrome information packets on

me, when they took Nella away to begin checking her for all the other things that could be wrong with her, and when the visitors would begin to leave that night and darkness would again set in just like it had done the night before, bringing with it the sadness demons. I was terrified of darkness.

I heard the phone ring and someone jumped to answer it. My friends were busy loving on Nella, laughing, filling the room with much-needed joy and playing their role of maintaining normalcy when Heidi handed me the phone. "It's your brother."

I had talked to Bubby the night before, but words were hardly spoken. Rather, we both gripped our phones, twelve hundred miles apart from each other, and sobbed convulsively for about ten minutes. I'll never forget hearing my brother cry. My strong brother who loved me cried like a child, whimpering, "I love you, I love you so much, Kas," and begging me to love her. He wanted to be with us so badly—I heard it in his voice, and I knew frequent phone calls would be important to both of us.

"Hi, Kas, how ya hangin' in there?" my brother mustered. He's called me Kas since I was little. It's the only name he calls me and, while I have no idea how the name came to be, it was comforting to hear that term of endearment in the midst of my sorrow. As makeshift-happy as the environment was for the time being, I couldn't help but begin to cry again when I heard my brother's voice. Others in the room sensed the change in my mood and grew quiet, still laughing and small-talking but lowering their volume out of respect and probably curiosity as to how I would respond.

"Bubby, I'm so sad. I'm just so, so sad." And when he heard me, he began to cry again.

"I know, Kas. I just can't stop thinking about you. I can't stop thinking about Nella and how much I love her. Dahna and I can't stop crying, can't stop talking about it, can't stop praying for you guys. Dad sent me a picture of her and I keep look—" His voice broke and we cried together, neither of us able to talk for a moment. As much as it hurt to hear he and my sister-in-law were so sad, it felt comforting to know my sorrow was shared. "Kas, I love her so much. Promise me you'll love her, okay?"

"Bubby, I do. I love her so much. I'm just so sad." I couldn't think of any other way to put it and as simple as that sentence was—*I'm so sad*—I repeated it relentlessly because it was all I could think of at the moment. I couldn't even tell you specifically what I was sad about. It was just overwhelming grief for the death of a dream, for the loss of the baby I thought I'd have.

"Kas, will you tell her her uncle loves her? Tell her I think she's awesome," he said.

"I will, Bubby."

"I want to get a tattoo that says *Nella*," he added.

"I think that would be great." I smiled and wiped my tears. I knew this wouldn't be the last I heard from him today. "I love you, Bubby."

"I love you too, Kas." And we hung up.

I looked up to see everyone completely frozen and staring, a common sight after moments like this, taking their cues from me as to what they should do. Was I going to break down, laugh, beg to hold her, scream at God, bury my head into the pillow, ask for some comedic relief? These moments happened often in that room, moments where everyone who was present was willing and ready to do whatever they needed to do to help lift me toward healing. They'd take my cues and follow, crying with me, holding me or, most often, coaching me toward happiness, throwing a joke in here and there, reminding me of my resounding purpose . . . to be me. To love my girls. To live life big. To carry on.

"You need to eat," someone chimed in again, repeating the famous four words I heard so often those first few days.

"I can't," I cried. And as quickly as I said it, a Styrofoam cup was shoved toward me, and Laura pushed a straw in my mouth, "Drink, babe. Drink this." She held the cup while I sucked some strawberry banana concoction that apparently was packed with protein and fat, and I tried not to think of it drowning me but rather strengthening me, providing magical courage and all the things I would need to pass on to Nella.

My Girl. She hadn't even been in this world half a day and yet she seemed so accustomed to this new life outside my belly. She started making little bird noises in my dad's arms and was quickly passed to me to nurse. That's the great thing about nursing. No matter who's holding your baby, you get to ask for the little one back for legitimate reasons every couple hours. I needed those moments. For as sad as I was, I couldn't help but swoon every time I held those six little pounds of love that needed me. That were made from my cells. That latched on and made breathy noises and grasped my fingers while I fed her.

While the fanfare in the room continued, I looked down at Nella as she ate and tried to see her as my baby—the same one who, just a few nights earlier, I referred to when I went to bed and told Brett, "Can you believe we'll be holding her in just a few days?" I studied her face and wondered what exactly it was that made her so different from what I had

imagined. Her nose was a little flattened, yes, but still tiny and cute. Her eyes were closed and had tiny blond lashes if you looked closely. Her ears were small and low but much cuter than some ears I had seen on newborns. Together, why did her features scream a diagnosis rather than a perfect newborn who smelled delicious and squeaked little baby peeps and nestled into the nook of my neck the way she had been made to do?

By the afternoon, a constant flow of friends had been coming and going, and my moods shifted like tides. I laughed when obvious moments presented themselves and cried when the sadness cloud suddenly reemerged. I couldn't help but laugh when Wylie's husband, Vinnie, entered my room for a visit only to find me nursing and he, startled and embarrassed, flung his body around to leave the room so fast he got tangled in the partition curtain, slapstick style. If that wasn't funny enough, Wylie left the room to chase him down, and we heard her scolding him in the hallway. "Vinnie!" she snapped. "Quit being so nervous! Now get in there, dammit! Just don't stare at her boobs!"

But as funny as many moments were, I helplessly yielded to the panic and suffocating sadness that would randomly take hold of me. At one point, I remember being huddled with a group of my friends on my bed, laughing and making small talk when, with no warning at all, I was overcome. I went from smiling to instant tears. "I can't believe this is happening to me," I cried. And my friends would swarm like bees, closer to me, touching me. "I know, I know. It's gonna be okay," they'd say.

Anyone can say "It's gonna be okay." It's really a line of total bullshit if you think about it, because no one really knows if it's gonna be okay or not. But, when you feel like you haven't a hope in the world and all the people you love are circling around you, holding you, chanting "It's gonna be okay," there is power in those words. When one person says it, it starts to feel good. When two people say it, you might even believe it. And when the masses are crowding around you, cheering you on—*It's gonna be okay, It's gonna be okay*—it becomes true. It really does.

WHEN BRETT BROUGHT LAINEY BACK UP, IT WAS PAINFUL to even look at her. I just felt as if I'd failed her so badly. I had all these dreams in my mind of what her sister relationship would be and all the things they would do together and I felt, at that moment, like they had been shattered. Would Lainey end up having to take care of her? Would they not share motherhood dreams and walk in each other's weddings? What did this mean for the sisterhood bond I had promised her—the one like I had? It almost made it worse that she had no idea, climbing happily in my lap to kiss her *Baby 'Ella,* and then hopping back down to investigate the room, completely oblivious to the sadness. I had packed a bag of toys for her and, despite the fact I wanted to pick her up and run, it was strangely comforting to have a sense of normalcy enforced with her sitting on the wood floor of that room, nurturing baby dolls, coloring in her Elmo book, mischievously pressing Play-Doh into hidden corners of hospital furniture.

And Brett? Oh, that man. That man I love. While I knew he loved Nella, while I knew her diagnosis didn't change a thing about the way he would treat her, I was scared to ask him about his sadness. I think everyone assumes you find the most comfort in moments like these in your spouse—that you run to them and beg them not to leave your side. It's not that I didn't find my comfort there. It's just that it was an unspoken comfort. We knew we both were hurting and there were definitely tearful hugs and calls and secret efforts we made to comfort each other, but I needed him home, making life for Lainey as normal and grand as it could be. My own sadness was about all I could deal with at the time, and I was having trouble as it was to balance that with being the best mama to our new girl, so we made unspoken decisions to support each other quietly, to love, to hug, to burrow into each other's shoulders and say "we can do this," but we both knew Brett's role was to carry on. He came every day to that room and stayed as long as I needed him. He held Nella and whispered soft daddy things in her ear. He called me and texted me and told me everything at home was just fine. And that's exactly what I needed to hear. I needed Home to be just fine because I was headed there

soon. Home is where this was actually all going to play out, and I needed it to be ready for us.

It was late in the afternoon when Brett was getting ready to take Lainey back home. She was bored with the four walls of that room, and there's only so many fun things a toddler can do with a puke bin, a canister of Tucks, and some frozen pads. (Don't even get me started on those frozen pads.) Brett sat behind me in my bed, and I leaned against his chest while a handful of girlfriends were keeping us company. The doctor covering my OB's rounds walked in, and I watched as my girlfriends all came to attention, for his good looks were not to go unnoticed.

"Hi, I'm covering for Dr. Alexander today. Just checkin' in on ya and seeing how you're doing. Is there anything you need?" He flashed a Hollywood grin and waited for a reply.

Hmmm. Anything I need? Oh, I don't know, a tranquilizer? My approach, less sarcastic, still pleaded for relief. "Is there anything I can have"—I paused, wondering how one might subtly raise an emotional SOS in an appropriate way to a hot doctor—"something where I can still nurse but that would help me not be so sad?" He, apparently unaware of our "situation," posed a puzzled look and continued.

"You mean you're just struggling with the new mom thing?" He tried to be diplomatic and respectful, but I realized he had no idea we'd just been hit by the emotional version of a Mack truck. Here he thought I was just overwhelmed by motherhood in general and wanted something to put me out of my misery.

"Oh, no," I corrected. "You see, we didn't know until she was born"—I paused for a moment; I was going to have to say it—"that she, um . . . she has Down syndrome."

It was the first time I said it out loud. Everyone else had said it for me up to this point.

Dr. Hottie smiled, swiftly adjusting his approach, softening his demeanor and beautifully volleying back with quick-witted humor. "Well, I guess there's always crack. Spacecakes. Mushrooms . . ."

The room suddenly filled with laughter. Loud, happy laughter from everyone. Leaning against Brett's chest, I felt his laughter as his body shook and his arms relaxed. It felt so healing, I hugged him even closer. Humor—the ever-present catalyst for normalcy in this current of *Life Moves On*. We still laugh.

Dr. Hottie offered a few scripts for some drugs but it would mean I'd have to stop nursing, and I wasn't willing to give that up. So I stuffed the scripts into my purse, hoping I'd never need them, and I thanked him for checking on us. Later, my nurse would tell me she saw him dancing once at a Christmas party and that he was a really good dancer and strangely, I'd never be able to think about this story in the hospital again without thinking of him rocking out his moves.

IT WAS EARLY AFTERNOON WHEN SHIFTS OF FRIENDS attending Room 16 began to change. New friends rolled in while tired ones who had been there all morning waved good-bye. I'll never forget the moment when, amid the good chaos of voices in Room 16 that day, I heard Heidi announce the good news.

"Kelle, your sister just landed," she said. "She's on her way."

the blue pill

MY SISTER WALKED THROUGH THE DOOR OF ROOM 16 that evening carrying one small bag, and when she entered, our eyes did not even meet. She looked only for Nella, scanning the room for the tiny bundle, dropping her bags, and running to hold her. Like I was viewing a slow-motion scene from a movie, I watched as she scooped her away from my friend, pressed her cheek closely against Nella's, squeezed her in tight, and wept. But they were not sad tears—they were grateful, happy tears, and anyone who was present to witness them knew it. "She's so precious," she whispered. "She's just so precious, Kelle." I smiled. There was no apology, no pity or sadness in her statement. And this is exactly why I wanted her here. She didn't come to soothe me, to hold my hand while I cried. She came to change me.

Carin and I grew up like any other sisters—sharing a room, fighting over clothes, tattling on each other over stupid things. She had an advantage in our fights though, with her razor-sharp claws that she used to swipe and run. I, on the other hand, bit my

nails and was therefore never a fair match. Other than our short-lived fighting period and the scratch scars I bore from it, we really were quite close. And then our parents' divorce brought us even closer. By the time she moved out and got married, I idolized her.

We're only a few years apart, but Carin has the experience and wisdom of an old soul, seasoned with myriad events many people don't face in an entire lifetime. She has three girls—Savannah, Sydney, and Somer—so she's been down this crazy road of loving little souls long before me. She knows things—like how to love your kids with everything you have and yet not go crazy when they're whining or kicking or not sleeping through the night. She's also given me the best tips on mothering I know—ones the books won't tell you. Like the best way to decompress is to put your kids to bed early, pour a glass of wine, toast an English muffin, and go climb in your car and rock out to some tunes. And thanks to her, I know how to cut my own bangs with a pair of kindergarten Fiskars. She's my Obi-Wan. And, although I joke about the silly things she's taught me, it's the important things I've really gained from her. Like how to love. And be confident. And enjoy this ride of life by making the best of everything it has to offer.

The year before Nella was born, my sister made the difficult decision to leave a tumultuous marriage. There are people who go through a divorce. And then there are people who *grow* through a divorce. My sister was the latter. She underwent an evolution of beauty and strength over that difficult year that truly shaped her into the wise and confident woman she is today. She struggled— oh, yes—learning the hard way just as much as the condensed 224-page self-help book way. But, through all the tearful conversations she had with me during that year, through all the "How can I do this?" pleas and "This is so hard," through counselors and lawyers and struggling to make it on her own with her girls, it wasn't long before I saw the reward of the trials in her life. It wasn't long before the pain of circumstances had polished her soul into something stronger, wiser, happier. Thank God she had her crash course in life just a year before mine. Because I needed her strength more than anything that day.

ABOUT THE TIME THAT CARIN ARRIVED TO HOLD HER new niece and fire up her emotional boot camp for me, we were informed that Nella's bilirubin counts were elevating, and we had to start the blue light therapy for jaundice. If there's one thing I was well versed in, it was jaundice. Lainey had a very unusual case of it right after she was born—one that put us in an ambulance to Fort Myers Hospital, extending our entire hospital stay to ten days past her birth. And, if there's one thing any mama who's gone through newborn jaundice can tell you, it's that it sucks not to be able to hold your baby when you've waited nine months just to touch her, labored God knows how long to push her out, and finally received your reward only to be told she has to lie blindfolded in a plastic light box in nothing but a diaper. Add to that the trauma of finding out the perfect baby you had expected has an extra chromosome, when you're struggling to bond and need every bit of sweet, breathy cradling time as it is, and . . . well, you get the picture. I was upset. Even managed, in the midst of my sorrow, to pick up a snarky attitude toward God. One of those "Oh, really, God? Jaundice, too?" kind of mind-sets. But, through the frustration and desperation, there was a huge moment of victory. Fifty percent of babies born with Down syndrome have congenital heart defects—many severe enough to require NICU stays and, eventually, open heart surgery. And, while jaundice wasn't exactly something I wanted to go through again, the bad news of blue lights and a blindfold was followed by the reassuring results of Nella's echocardiogram. Her heart was . . . *perfect*.

I wonder if subconsciously I was waiting to hear this news before I let myself truly bond with her. If, in my deep pain, I was worried we'd be told something worse—something that might take her away from us—and so I was protecting myself from being hurt any more. What I do know is that between my sister's arriving, hearing the news of our baby's healthy heart, watching the nurses roll in light carts and rigging up the station where Nella would lie for the next few days—between the steady stream of friends and family that came to see us that day and the phone calls and the social workers who sat in our room and told us they knew someone who knew someone this has happened to and they're just

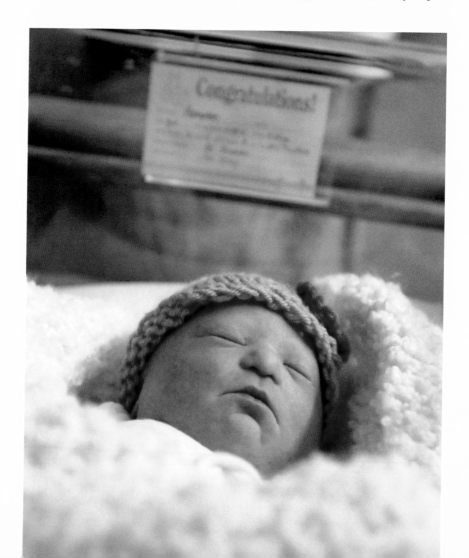

fine—between all of that, I began to feel it. I began to feel this throbbing love for my daughter and the need to protect her and hold her and figure this thing out.

But I couldn't ignore the pain. At 4:24 P.M., it had officially been twenty-four hours since Nella made her way into the world, and yet it felt like days. With my sister there, I knew "the talk" was coming—the speech she had probably already delivered in her head on the plane ride down—but it wasn't time yet. The room was still filled with friends and nurses, with my dad and Brett, and Lainey, who found an Enfamil bottle in a drawer and determinedly crammed it into Nella's mouth despite her wincing and obvious distaste for formula. "That's okay," Brett told her, "I like boobies too."

By late afternoon, the room had taken on the feeling of comfort someone's new house has after it's been broken in. There were pillows on the floor, afghans from home sprawled over the couch, and my friends and my sister curled up like cats in every corner of the room. The lavender oil still burned, the candles still flickered, and the white noise of the blue light machine drowned out the cold stillness a hospital room might have had under any other circumstance. The irony of my unsettled heart in the midst of such settled comfort didn't go unnoticed. But the best part was when Brett swung open the door holding a cooler and a bag of limes.

"Guess what I got, babe?" He smiled his sheepish grin and gave the cooler a little shake.

My girlfriends screamed in unison, "BEER!"

"Oh God, I'm so in love with you," Laura told him as she reached out and grabbed the cooler. My husband might not always know what to do in a crisis, but he damn well knows how to drive to the corner store and pick up a six-pack. And sometimes, that's exactly what a crisis calls for.

I hadn't had a beer in nine months, and suddenly, I remembered what I was missing. I wanted the cold tang of a limey brew. I wanted my hands to hug the sculpted neck of a brown bottle. But really, I wanted a buzz, a dizzying buzz that might mask the pain for just a little bit. I looked up for my friend Dot's approval. Dot's a nurse, and when she said a nursing mama can certainly have a beer and that, hell—it might even help your milk come in, I covered her sticker of approval over my guilt and stashed away her permission like ammunition, ready to fire it out at anyone who questioned me. She handed me a beer, and I decided I would snap back with a nasty "Oh yeah? Dot said I could" if anyone even raised an eyebrow.

And so we drank, we laughed, we cried. It felt like so many other times we had bonded when my sister came to visit. Like the time a year

earlier we circled around the table at Sam Snead's, our favorite bar, licking buffalo wing sauce off our fingers, ordering another round, and listening as we each went around sharing pains and triumphs and, ultimately, some hilariously funny shit. I've always loved the way my sister lives twelve hundred miles away and yet, when she's here, you'd never know it. My friends know her from my stories, from the times she's been down here, and now when she comes, they embrace her as a long-lost friend, picking up where we all left off.

While there was no bar table or basket of buffalo wings in Room 16, there was a bed. And a couch. And between the two of them, we huddled together as my sister finally shifted gears from purposefully funny to purposefully serious. The fun stuff? The laughing? It was the beginning act, and the stage was slowly prepping now for the real deal.

"I want you to listen to a song," she said. "I keep thinking of it—ever since Dad called me last night, and I want you to hear it." My sister's a lyrics buff. She declares new anthems through every phase of her life and spent three months of her divorce pounding her feet to the pavement as she ran out her stresses to the beats and truths of songs with powerful lyrics. And in doing so, her brain has become a virtual library of music—songs that she's able, at a moment's notice, to pull out for any pertinent theme. We clambered to my laptop that Brett had brought up to the hospital to keep me busy, but the hospital's network had a firewall that wouldn't let us listen to music. Still, we would not be deterred. Within seconds, my problem-solving friend Kelly had YouTube pulled up on her phone and cranked up the volume. And we sat—about six of us—huddled around that phone she held in the back corner of the hospital room and listened to the words of Sara Groves's "Add to the Beauty" . . . and wept. Right before I listened, I ran over to the blue light box where my girl was sleeping, scooped her up, and peeled her blindfold off. I wanted to be holding her for the beginnings of my soul stretching. And so I held her in my arms and looked down at her sweet face—at her tiny smooshed nose and almond eyes, and I listened to these words:

We come with beautiful secrets.
We come with purposes written on our hearts,

Written on our souls.

We come to every new morning with possibilities

Only we can hold...

Redemption comes in strange places, small spaces

Calling out the best of who we are.

And I remember at that point—those very first few lines—something breaking inside me, like a dam releasing the floodwaters held behind it. All the emotion I had been holding through our previous laughter broke through and warm tears began to flow, slowly dripping into puddles on Nella's cheeks. And it hurt again, so deeply. The I-can't-believe-this-is-happening-to-us feeling reemerged and with it came deep, concentrated pain. I pulled her in closer to my chest, at this point unable to control my shaking sobs, and continued to listen. . .

And I want to add to the beauty
To tell a better story

I want to shine with the light

That's burning up inside...

Redemption comes in strange places, small spaces

Calling out the best of who we are ...

This is grace, an invitation to be beautiful

... an invitation ...

Calling out our best...

The song ended and I looked around. Everyone was a mess. Nella's poor face had basically had a tear bath, and my body was finally settling after it had just lost a battle with an ugly cry. But those words—oh, those words. What did it all mean? As confused as I may have been, I knew exactly what it meant.

I noticed from our window in the room that the sun was setting, and I watched as friends began gathering their things, ready to leave us alone with my sister. I, once again, made my painful good-byes with Lainey, watched as Brett gathered her things, preparing to leave, and made a mental note that this was now the longest I had ever been away from her—two nights. And then, I started to panic. The darkness demons were returning. They had won the fight the night before, trampling me with their sadness and despair, and I could taste their pain in the room again as the sunlight from the windows slowly disappeared. I writhed in bed, whimpering like a child.

"It's getting dark," I cried. "I can't do this again. I hate the darkness, the sadness . . ." My voice trailed off, mumbling panicked cries.

"It's okay," my sister assured. "It will get better every night."

I looked over at Nella, sleeping soundly in the blue light isolette, and I glanced at the clock, wondering if it was time for her to eat again. I wanted to hold her. I wanted her out from under the lights and I didn't want to wait for the only time I was supposed to take her out. Twenty more minutes. I looked again and my heart throbbed. "Aw, screw it," I decided. "I'll feed her early."

Our suggested twenty-minute feeding outside the light therapy turned into forty-five minutes of good, rule-breaking snuggling while my sister and Heidi and I passed her back and forth before we finally returned her to the blue glow of her bed. I had asked Heidi to stay again and she willingly obliged. In fact, she even arranged for her husband to bring an Italian feast up to the hospital late that night. Jeff was leaving a catered party that had some hefty leftovers, so he dropped by with two platters of lasagna and baked ziti, a portable DVD player, and a stash of feel-good movies, my favorite—*You've Got Mail*—among them. Combined with our beer cooler, it made for a comforting evening.

It's hard to describe the room that night, but something transformed. While the sky was black outside, our room glowed from the blue light on the far end of the room and the numerous candles that flickered in every corner. Heidi popped in a movie on the DVD player, and even though we didn't watch it, its comforting sounds hummed in the background—like the sound track to a sleepover. The room smelled inviting, not at all like a hospital, but homey, with the scent of a good Italian meal wafting from our smorgasbord. And, for the first time in over two days, I ate. I piled my plate high with pasta, cracked open a beer, and leaned comfortably against my pillow on the bed, making room for Carin and Heidi to join me, and the three of us ate and drank and laughed like summer camp cabinmates.

"Mom's coming Monday," Carin informed me. "She got her ticket today." I smiled. I knew Carin couldn't stay long—in fact, she was only here for one night before she had to get back to her girls—but my mom would be here to pick up the pieces just like she's always done. I knew my mom was unfazed by this, that the call she received and the two words that changed my life did nothing more to her than make her hurt for *me*. I knew, to Mom, this was no big deal—just a little something extra to love—and that at that very moment she was probably crocheting something fierce to finish another lavish gift for the new granddaughter she couldn't wait to meet.

One of the nurses peeked her head in to check on us. "You need any-thing?" she asked. She looked around the room and smiled as she no-ticed the beer, the Italian feast, the way we were all cross-legged on the bed talking. "Looks like you're all set. You girls have fun," she said with a wink, closing the door behind her. I felt like we were fourteen, staying at a friend's house, and she was just the really cool mom who made sure we were enjoying ourselves. Maybe she'd be back with some Capri Suns and Bagel Bites if we were lucky.

And, suddenly, without notice, they came again—the sadness de-mons. I didn't see them coming this time with my little beer buzz and my short-lived happy façade, but they came in, those sneaky demons. They came in fast before I could block them, and I took a good slap to the face and a punch to the gut so that, within seconds, I was hunched over my plate of food, crying while the demons snickered victoriously in the corner. They had won again, leaching my strength from me, my courage.

I can't believe this is happening.

And that's when it came. Carin's speech. The speech I will forever remember. The "I Have a Dream" speech, I now call it. The one that was delivered by flickering candles, late on a Saturday night, to a sad girl hunched over a plate of baked ziti who thought life would never be the same. The one that began to change me.

"Kelle, I know you can't see through this now," Carin began, "and that's okay, because you just can't and you won't for a little while, but *I* can and this makes so much sense to me. You were made for this role. You were. I truly believe you were chosen for this and it makes *so* much sense."

And I knew. Tears rolled down my cheeks as I nodded my head. *Yes, yes, I know.* "You know," she continued, "hard times are so good for people. Not everyone gets to go through them, but the ones who do—" She stopped for a moment, and I knew the things she was about to say were pertinent to her own struggles just as much as mine. "I keep picturing a river with this crazy rushing current," she continued. "You can hang on and get exhausted struggling to just stay alive, stuck to that rock, or you can let go and be carried by where it's going to take you. You have to let go, Kelle."

I had no words. I just kept nodding yes. *Yes, yes, I know.*

My sister was smiling. She was smiling and crying at the same time and as she talked, she leaned forward, excited. Carin is a petite little thing, a porcelain doll with short blond hair who gets carded every time she tries to buy a drink and yet from this small girl, a much greater truth was unfolding.

"I just want to go back," I cried. "I want to go back and be pregnant again so bad. I want it to be yesterday morning when I was happy."

"I know you do," my sister said, "but you can't go back. You can't go back, Kelle. You swallowed the blue pill, and there's no going back. You can look at that bag of clothes from yesterday all you want and cry because you were happy then, but it's not going to do anything for you. You're allowed to be sad. But you are eventually going to have to get up and move. Go for a walk. Put makeup on. Do all the actions that tell yourself you are moving forward with life."

Heidi and I were both crying and she took a moment to open the cooler, a moment of relief, to pull another beer out, twist the cap off, and hand it to me. Girl knows how to be a friend.

"I know you're right," I cried. "I know I was chosen. I just miss that

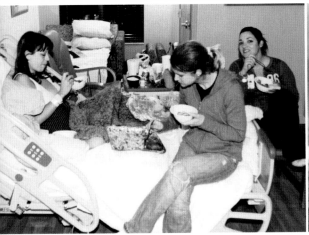

baby I never got to meet. I just want this sadness to go away. I don't want to be *that family*. I don't want people to feel sorry for us. I don't want Lainey to be sad. What did I do to her?" I thought of my little blond pixie, probably sleeping at home, and I was gripped with sadness for her.

"Kelle, there's always a plus side," Carin continued. "Lainey might not call Nella for her chicken casserole recipe, but she'll be changed in ways she wouldn't be otherwise. And just like I could be sad that my kids aren't benefiting from me being a stay-at-home mom right now, I have to look at what they are getting—a good role model for work ethic and independence. While Lainey might not have what you wished for her, she'll have many things other siblings will never get to know. This will be all Lainey will ever know, and she will love it and not wish to change it for anything someday."

My sister told me she wished I could see what she saw—because what she saw was wonderful. She said I was lucky—that I'd been offered a shortcut to what life is all about when some people search for it their whole lives and never know. She said I had a secret—a secret to happiness and that, while people may look at me and pity me, in time I'd feel like I knew something they didn't. "Someday, Kas," she said, "you'll feel so happy in spite of their pity glances. And you'll wish so badly you could let them know—that you could show them what life is about."

It was a lot to take in, but it was so good. I wanted a pencil—to jot it all down in a notebook like an eager student, craving knowledge. I wanted to paint her words on the ceiling so I could see them at night and to record her voice so I could play it back when I knew I'd falter in weeks to come. Nella was stirring from the blue lit corner, and Carin leaped to rescue her. But she wasn't finished. She handed me my girl, and she went on.

"You know, through pain, you learn a lot about yourself—things you thought you never knew you wanted to learn. And it's kind of like those animals that regrow a part of their body—like starfish. You might not feel it now. You might not even want to grow, but you will. You'll grow the part that broke off, and that growing, that blooming—cannot happen without the pain.

"We're all conditioned by society about what is good, desirable, normal, and what is bad. The sadness that you're feeling right now is only because of conditioning. Don't let society determine how you feel. Kelle, you can reshape the conditioning for the rest of the world." She stopped for a moment, as if she was not just enlightening me, but herself as well.

"Life is like a choose-your-own-adventure book. I thought I'd be on page 68 today, but look . . . I'm not. I'm divorced and starting over. And you thought you'd be at page 71 today, but you're on page 49 instead. And it's a whole different ending than you thought it would be, but you get to take it from here. It will still end well—you'll just take a little bit of a different route."

Holding Nella during these words did something for me. I actually began to get excited. The pain was still there, taking up a big part of my heart, but it was time for Pain to get a roommate. It wasn't happy about sharing a room, but Pain is never really happy. When Change came through the door that day, moving Pain's belongings to the side, confining it to only half of my heart's space, it brought with it a new perspective. Change starts small—a bit shy at first. But slowly Change does great things. Change renovates new spaces and places into something beautiful. And that's just something Pain was going to have to deal with.

By this time, we were so deep into this beautiful conversation, there were laughter and smiles to keep the tears company. Empty beer bottles were scattered in between flower vases and diapers, and we decided, soon after midnight, to go after second helpings of our party food. Before we moved on to more laughter, Carin delivered her final words.

"So many people fear hard times," she said, "they go through their life solely seeking comfort and avoiding personal growth at all costs because it hurts. But I promise you, Kelle. I promise—if you can find a part of you to believe me and trust what I'm saying—you *will* be happier than you've ever been. There will come a day when you believe everything I'm saying from the deepest part of your soul, and it will be real and true. That's growth. I want you to picture some hypothetical person in your mind—someone who handled Down syndrome exactly like you wish you could. Now go and be that person. Rock this out, Kelle. Rock it out and show the world another way. Imagine a light switch in your brain—a switch that shifts your paradigm. Put on different glasses, discard the old ones, and flip the switch, Kelle. Because life is all about how you look at it."

And then she was done. I half expected her to collapse after her speech as if she was just yielding to a higher power, the courier of a mystical message meant to be delivered. But she didn't. She joined in second plates of ziti, in snuggling with Nella who was awake and being passed among loving arms, and in the laughter and healing power that filled that room. It was . . . *magical.* And there was no trace of the sadness demons, for the power of the perspective in the room that evening was far more than they could handle. So off they went. And when the trail of dust they left cleared, if you looked closely, you could see it . . . a small green bud. Something magnificent was growing.

chapter 5

homecoming

WITH MY SISTER IN MY ROOM THAT NIGHT AND
MY best friend by my side, I felt I could let go a bit—maybe
even get some sleep. I hadn't really slept since the night before
Nella was born, and I knew if I was going to try and adopt a new
attitude, sleep was where it would start. The thing was, Nella
wasn't happy under the blue lights anymore. Two days into her
life, she figured out it's far more fun being snuggled in someone's arms than lying in a box, and she kept wiggling out of
her blindfold so her little eyes were staring into light, and then
she'd fuss and wiggle some more. I jumped up every ten minutes to comfort her for the first hour of the night, but Carin
and Heidi soon banished me to my bed and said they'd take the
night shift. I remember falling back asleep and yet being very
aware of their giggling in the corner.

"This is bullshit," Carin complained. "Why can't we just hold
her? She hates it alone under that box."

"We'll get in trouble," Heidi answered.

"So?" Carin shot back. "I don't care. She needs touch."

And then I heard more giggling, more stifled laughter, and some crashing around. Curious, I rolled over and opened my eyes to find the greatest MacGyver stunt of all time. There was a rocking chair under the lights—the lights that had been rigged up to hang over Nella's bed. And in that chair sat Heidi, perfectly upright, half asleep, wearing a pair of sunglasses, completely illuminated by a blue glow, like a character from a science fiction movie. She had shimmied into the rocking chair pushed under the light box and was holding in her lap a little naked Nella who was perfectly content, sleeping on a pillow, getting the best of both worlds—loving arms and the blue light she needed. Heidi and Carin would swap this position throughout the entire night, laughing every time they traded shifts, knocking things over, and *sshhh*ing each other to keep the nurses at bay. But my girl was kept happy while I slept. And although I maybe only got about four hours of sleep that night, by the time the welcoming sun lit up our room the next morning, I felt like a new person.

At 7:00, the nurses' shift had changed, and I knew what that meant. Shauna would be here. Shauna had been my nurse two and a half years earlier when I stayed in this very same place to welcome Lainey, and she'd quickly become my favorite. Shauna is pretty and kind. She has a thick southern drawl that's comforting and friendly, and her kind demeanor has a way of melting new mama anxieties like butter on hot peach pie. She consoles like a mama, taking care of her patients

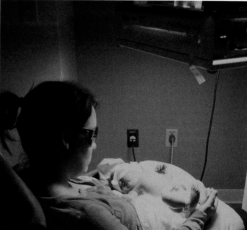

like kindred spirits, and if you've ever wished Paula Deen was your grandma like I have, then you'd surely wish Shauna was your friend. The Friday we had checked in to deliver Nella, I saw Shauna walking out of the hospital and so I ran, holding my big pregnant belly as if the baby would fall out if I didn't, and chased her down. I had already found out through a friend of a friend that she'd be working the following Sunday, and it was all arranged she'd be assigned to me. So I gave her a quick hug, told her I was so excited she'd be my nurse again, and made some sort of cheesy comment about how next time she'd see me, I'd be holding a baby.

As the sun creeped up and the unit awakened with the new shift, I knew Shauna would be walking in soon. And, as it had been with every new face I encountered since "this happened," I started to get sad again, as if the old me and the new me were completely separate entities, as if I had to reintroduce myself every time I saw someone from my past and start relationships from scratch. I figured Shauna would have been prepped with my chart before she walked in the room—that nurses had huddled in the nurses' station and whispered about the mom who had an unexpected Down syndrome birth. I imagined there was a red sticker on the cover of my chart that said "Warning: Very Sad Mom. Tread with Caution." And then I wondered what happened next. If Shauna's heart sank with disappointment, if she felt sorry for me, if she didn't know what to say before she walked into that room.

But she didn't need to say anything. When she walked in that morning, her warm eyes met mine and the dam broke again. I couldn't speak—just cried, and Shauna came to my bedside, reached down, and hugged me tight and didn't let go. I laid my head on her shoulder and cried like she was my mom. Her hair was soaking up my tears, and I was comforted by the fact that her perfume smelled just like the one my aunt Esther wears. And when we pulled away, Shauna smiled and offered me the happiest, most southern, sunshiney "Congratulations." The only thing that would have topped that moment is if Paula Deen herself walked in and whipped us up some biscuits and gravy that morning.

The troops began arriving again, but this time it felt like they weren't just there to comfort me—they were there to have fun. The nurses laughed that Room 16 was the party room and said, "My, you must be a lucky girl to have so many loved ones." My sister left, but my mom arrived, bringing with her homemade gifts for my girls and her sense of humor. My mom doesn't try to be funny. It just happens on its own. Like when she pointed to the painting hanging over my hospital bed—the one with a beautiful mother holding two children—and her eyes lit up and she excitedly announced, "Kelle! Look! Those children in that painting look like they might have Down syndrome. That's so neat!" And the fact that she's serious and really thinks this just might be an act of God—some sort of divine coincidence—sends my girlfriends and I into rolling-on-the-floor fits of laughter. But that's just my mom.

The fact that the mood had changed, that we laughed and bonded,

that things took on a lighthearted beauty, didn't mean we were naive about our new circumstances. Within hours of Nella's birth, I had
a crash course in Down syndrome and all the health issues involved. I
could have easily been paralyzed with fear, but I'm not the kind of person who can handle that kind of mind-set. As my dad always says, "Don't
let your worries for tomorrow rob your joys of today." At the fork in the
road on this journey, I thought long and hard before I chose my path.
And, for the sake of everyone—but especially my kids, who needed a
happy mama—I took the path of positivity.

Having the most amazing pediatrician surely helped as well. When
Dr. Foley came to check on us on Day Three, I was ready for her visit.
Another warm and friendly soul, Dr. Foley's known me long enough to
understand what kind of mama I am and how I like things presented to
me. She's patient with my craziness and formulates the answers to my
questions carefully and comfortingly.

"So, I know her heart is okay," I began, "but what else do I need to
worry about? Can she hear okay? Will she need glasses? Does she have
to have lots of tests?"

Dr. Foley smiled, accustomed to my barrage of questions.

"Kelle, she's perfectly healthy," she stated simply. "Right now, you
just love her. And she is doing so great. She's eating like a champ and lots
of babies with Down syndrome have problems sucking. You're already
over a lot of the struggles lots of other moms have to face."

She was right. Our girl had a healthy heart, she passed her hearing
test, and she sucked like a Hoover vacuum. What more could you ask for?

After I pressed her a little more, Dr. Foley told me about the thyroid test we'd have to do every six months ("which is no big deal," she
added), about the eye exam we'd do later ("If she has to wear glasses,
I'll find the cutest damn glasses this side of the Mississippi," I told
her), and about the decreased muscle tone that, according to Dr. Foley,
"just makes her more snuggly." While I braced myself for the most
godawful things I could possibly be told, I was pleasantly surprised.
And completely comforted when, after I made some comment about

Nella kind of being like other "normal" babies, Dr. Foley jumped in and corrected me. "Kelle, stop saying that. She *is* normal. She's a normal baby. She just has this thing called Down syndrome like some babies have asthma or some kids have other things. She's a normal, perfect, beautiful baby. And I'm here to help you with all the medical things you'll need to know."

I cried again. Those tear ducts of mine were truly impressive—fully capable of making tears when you'd think they were done and dried up. "You know," I told her, "I'm gonna do this differently than you've ever seen it done before. I'm gonna come up with my own way, and it's gonna be amazing."

Dr. Foley smiled. "Kelle, I wouldn't expect anything less." Oh, I love that woman.

She told me they did a blood test for chromosomal studies—just to confirm the Down syndrome, but that she was pretty certain Nella had that magical extra chromosome and not to worry about the test. And before she left the room, she scooped Nella up and hugged her just like she always does in her nonclinical way—in a way that endears her to me not just as a doctor but as a woman, as a mother, as an individual who understands the human spirit and the emotional battles we face when we welcome life. And for that, I'm thankful.

IF DAY ONE WAS FOR PAIN AND DAY TWO WAS FOR CHANGE, then Day Three was for embracing not only a new perspective, but the support that was unfolding from everyone we'd ever known. My brother called again, for probably the fifth time, but this time there was no crying, no still silence while we both sniffled and caught our breath. This time, he was excited. Heidi answered the phone again and handed it to me smiling, "It's your brother again."

"Hi, Bubby," I said.

"Hey, Kas." I could hear the smile in his voice. "How's that little niece of mine?"

I looked over at the blue light bed where she had comfortably settled in. "She's doing great. Eating awesome. Her bili counts are still a little high, but Dr. Foley said she expects them to go down in a couple days. We might have to stay a little longer though."

"I wish I was there, Kas. We'd have a party, you know."

Yes, if there's one thing Crydermans know how to do, it's party. I imagined if the whole family were here, my dad would have found a way to rig up a disco ball over my bed. My brother would have taught all the nieces some of the hilarious interpretive dance moves he's made up to whip out at the occasional wedding, and they'd all be chanting, "Nell-a rocks. Nell-a rocks." My mom would be shaking her head in the background mumbling some sort of embarrassed, "Oh, you guys. You're ridiculous," and my sister would be finding a way to pipe in some Sister Sledge over speakers she'd MacGyvered out of wire and batteries. Then the cousins would roll in—laughing, slapping one another on the back, taking turns holding Nella, and pouring everyone drinks. Lainey would be beaming, Brett would be attempting to hide one of his "your-family-is-so-cool" smiles, and all would be right with the world. Yes, if only Bubby were here.

"Kas, I'm gettin' really excited for you, and I have to admit, I'm actually a little bit jealous. I wish Nella was mine. You're going to know things none of us ever get to know. So, I'm really jealous."

I knew he wasn't saying this to patronize me. No, Bubby hates pity. He said it because he meant it.

"Kas, I have this vision," he continued, "and I know it's going to be true. Nella is going to bring our family together like never before. She's going to be the life of the party. Years from now, I can see it. If we all get together, everyone's gonna ask, 'Is Nella gonna be there?' and if she isn't, we'll be disappointed. I picture Christmas Eve at my house and everyone's there—" The tone in his voice was elevating, excited and passionate, gaining momentum like a sportscaster in the middle of a great play. He was talking fast and furious, and I couldn't help but gain a bit of his elated fever.

"Everyone's gonna be there, and there's gonna be lights and Christmas music and a fire in the fireplace," he said, "and we're all going to be laughing. And I can see Nella. She's going to have pigtails and some awesome jeans and a cool rocker tee. And let her wear Converse, okay? She needs some cool Converse tennis shoes. And, Kas, she's gonna be rockin' out on *Guitar Hero*. And we're all gonna be screamin', 'Go, Nella, Go!' and she's gonna be really good at that game. We're all going to laugh because she's jumpin' up and down playing songs and we're all singing along. Kas, it's gonna be awesome."

Once again, I couldn't speak. Tears familiarly rolled down my cheeks, except this time they stopped at the corners of my mouth that were turned up into the world's biggest, most healing smile.

I don't think I've ever loved my brother more. What he gave me at that moment was honest hope—hope that was so real, I felt like I could touch it.

The Net was in full force as well. Heidi had left the hospital room for all of about two hours a day to go spend some time with her kids and maybe sneak away to put them to sleep, and the rest of my friends came in constant shifts—with coffee, bagels, flowers, magazines, and the most valued of gifts—normalcy. We talked about Down syndrome, yes. In fact, my friends kept saying how excited they were to bring something new to our group—to have the opportunity to experience the beauty of differences up close and personal—to give their kids a chance to truly learn acceptance and love in different ways by having Nella as a friend. But we also talked about the cool boots that were on sale at Dillard's, who got kicked off *American Idol,* and whose mother-in-law was being particularly annoying.

Around Day Four, a system had been worked out where my friends, most of whom are teachers, would divvy up who went home to check on the kids first and who went straight to the hospital. Then they would switch. And on a quiet day one afternoon when everyone was working and my room had settled down with just my dad and Brett keeping me company for a while, I checked my phone to find an e-mail from my friend Theresa. I met Theresa through another friend, had taken pictures of her kids a couple of times, and only recently had really begun to know her to the point of calling her my own friend, and a wonderful one. The subject line: *Thinking of You.*

Dear Kelle,

I'm at school trying to teach . . . I keep losing my thoughts as they return to you and your new little, Nella. This is odd for me, usually my thoughts are with my kids . . . but today they are with you and yours. Not only do you have my thoughts, but you also have my heart and all the love in it. You need it more than I . . . keep it while yours is breaking, use mine to help repair yours . . . I trust you with it and I know that you'll return it when you no longer need it.

I will leave you with my heart and thoughts . . . and try to teach.

Today, because of you, I will teach: compassion, understanding, and love.

Love, xoxo Theresa

And suddenly, a rush of love for my friends came over me so strongly, I felt humbled to the point of tears. Theresa put it best—they had literally given me their hearts while mine was broken. They were slowly repairing me—and would continue to do so—by loving my girl. By continual visits with coffee and flowers, and midnight phone calls, consoling my tears. They all promised they were in it for the long haul—and were happy and honored to be part of the journey.

Julie, another friend of mine and the fifth-grade teacher who introduced me to Brett, called me in the hospital that same afternoon. Julie contains her emotions well. She's an incredible Italian cook, she's funny and loud, and yet the ones who know her well know she has a soft core of pure pudding. She'd do anything for anyone, and she was at a loss as to how she could help me. And, although I had left my teaching career a few years back, I was still closely connected to the many wonderful teachers and friends I had made at Pelican Marsh Elementary, and Julie was my connection to my old teaching world there.

"Do you mind if I send something out to the staff to let them know about Nella?" she asked.

"That would be great," I answered. The more people who knew meant a bigger support system for us and one less group of people with whom I'd worry about sharing the news.

"I also wondered if it would be okay if I organized a month of meals for you guys. I just want to do something for you," she added.

My eyes welled up. I could hear her voice cracking and knew how happy it would make her if she could do anything to heal my hurting heart. And if there's one thing Julie knows how to do, it's how to throw together some kick-ass meals.

"That would be wonderful," I said. "Julie, thank you so much."

She told me she'd send me the e-mail she put together before she sent it out for my approval. Later in the day, she sent this:

With great joy, Kelle Cryderman (Hampton) gave birth to Nella Cordelia Hampton on Friday, January 22, 2010, at 4:24 P.M. Baby Nella weighed 6 pounds and was 19 inches long. Mother and baby are happy and healthy.

I had a hard time reading through my tears. I knew another paragraph was coming and yet, with what I had read so far, I was already a mess. It seemed so real to see it in print. So matter-of-fact. I read on, my vision blurred with tears. . .

> Sometimes with each new blessing, life brings us new challenges. Baby Nella was born with Down syndrome. Although unexpected, we know that this blessing was given to Kelle because of her huge heart of gold and her love of life. If anyone can give this child the love and life she deserves, it is Kelle and Brett.
>
> Stephanie and I will be organizing meals for her in the near future. I will send out an e-mail and will post a calendar in the mail room.
>
> Kelle sends her love to all and will proudly be bringing Nella to visit soon.
>
> ~Julie

It was the most perfect e-mail I had ever read, and I knew how difficult it must have been for Julie to write it. I couldn't text her fast enough to tell her it was beautiful and so well-written, and I cried when she texted back, simply: *It was the hardest thing I've ever had to write. I wanted it to be perfect. Because you and Nella are perfect.*

After five days and an extended jaundice stay, it was time to go home. At first I was frustrated that we had to stay longer because my broken heart craved home so badly, but I realized later I needed more time in that hospital. Seeds that are started in clay pots need time to stretch their roots a little, to sprout the beginnings of a stem before they're transplanted to the ground where they will continue their growth. And so it was. The five days of grieving and beginning to grow in Room 16 were vital before I journeyed home.

From the moment Nella was born and we were told she had Down syndrome, Brett's first and only concern was, "Well, we can take her home, can't we?" As my dad says, "Home is Brett's Command Central,

the bridge of his USS *Enterprise*," and yes, he's right. Brett figures out everything from home, and for him, everything would fall into place once we pulled into the driveway. He was intent upon arranging pink balloons and a giant stork in the yard that said "Welcome Home, Nella!" He wanted the biggest celebration possible, and for that I love him.

It was bittersweet, really, packing up and getting ready to go home. So much had happened in that place, it was beginning to feel like sacred ground, and I knew that I would never be able to walk into that hospital again—to visit anyone—without feeling a guttural lurch in my stomach and my heart for what I had experienced here. I knew I had only just begun to process the last several days, and going home would mean this was real. My mom had crocheted Nella's going-home outfit and I had run my fingers over its fine handiwork so many nights before, it felt strange stretching it over our tiny baby's head when the situation wasn't exactly as I thought it would be. But still, she was beautiful—her skin tan and golden from the remaining jaundice and her features tiny as ever. While

I waited for Brett to pack the car up, I snapped as many pictures as I could of my sleeping girl all dressed up in the beautiful winter white dress my mom had spent so many hours crocheting. A snug little bonnet was tied around her pretty head and the smallest crocheted ballet slippers you've ever seen were tied with satin ribbon around her thin little ankles. This was it. We were going to do this now.

My dad stayed in the room with me and made sure I didn't get too sad. He pulled off the TANNING BOOTH sign he had made, the one he had taped to the jaundice lights, and handed it to me. "Keepsake. You might want this," he said. That initiated a scan of the room where my dad and I grabbed just about anything that wasn't nailed down to the floor for a memento of what we knew was a life-changing stay. He pretended to pull off the portrait hanging over the bed with the mother and the children who apparently looked like they had Down syndrome. "Think your mom might want this?" he teased, and we both laughed.

My nurse, Maria, another beautiful soul who comforted me with her kind and loving words of encouragement, came in to see if we needed any help. She brought with her an intern, a young and pretty girl, probably fresh out of college, and I wondered what she had likely been told before she walked into our room. Surely, this was probably the first time she'd dealt with this in her career, and I smiled to think our Nella could help teach a nurse, at the beginning of her work, a little bit about compassion. I wondered how many times she'd face this challenge again and if she'd remember us when she did.

Moments before we walked out of that room, I sat holding Nella in her beautiful outfit, taking in the last bits of our hospital experience, when a woman walked in. She was wearing scrubs, so I assumed she was a nurse, and she was beautiful, a Latina woman with long black hair and a thin build. She wore hot pink lipstick, and it outlined her radiant smile like a picture frame.

"I came to see this handmade outfit everyone's been talking about," she exclaimed, and she lovingly looked down at Nella and the fine handiwork her dress displayed. "She's beautiful," she said, and I thought I caught her voice cracking. I looked up to see tears, and a genuine smile. But there was something more.

The woman knelt down next to me and held my hand. Her grasp was warm and kind, and I found myself crying again.

"I have to tell you something," she whispered. Her beautiful Spanish accent was thick and pronounced, turning her words into poetry. "No one else knows," she continued. "I heard the nurses talking about this woman with a baby with Down syndrome and I thought I must come see."

She gripped my hand a little tighter, and her smile deepened.

"You are . . . so lucky," she said, "so very, very lucky."

I smiled, warm tears rolling, and nodded. *Yes, yes. We are lucky.* I leaned down and kissed Nella's cheeks while a tear rolled off onto her forehead and I quickly brushed it off.

"You see," she continued, "I was you one day long ago. I too had a very special baby just like yours. A little girl. And I wanted her so very much. Everything was pink"—she laughed and waved her arms in the air—"the room, the clothes. I couldn't wait. And when she was born, they told us that our baby too had Down syndrome." She rolled the "r" in *syndrome* so beautifully that for the first time, the word sounded pretty, magical . . . poetic. "But, you see—" She stopped for a moment and wiped her tears. "Our baby didn't make it. She was sick. And I would have done anything to keep her. I would have done anything to be in your place." She looked down at Nella and touched her cheek. "So I just want you to know, you are a very, very lucky woman. And she is beautiful."

I thanked her. Just wept and wiped hot tears and repeated, "Thank you. Thank you. Thank you." And then she walked out, disappearing like it had all just happened in my head. Had my dad not been there to witness it, I really would have questioned if it had indeed happened. But it did. And that woman has no idea just how much what she said that day meant to me.

Moments later, Brett appeared smiling, holding an empty car seat in one hand and a proud little girl wearing a "Big Sister" crown in the other. Together, we placed our new baby in that seat and I watched as Daddy tucked her in, checking the straps, tightening the buckle just as proud new daddies do. And I squeezed Lainey's hand while she held the car seat handle with the other, helping Brett as he walked. It was, strangely, just how I had imagined it would be. We all were smiling, nurses were congratulating us as we walked down the hallway, and my dad was furiously snapping pictures behind us.

I turned back once more before we stepped into the car and looked back at the place that had held so much sorrow. I took my fair share home with me, of course, but the worst of it—the heaviest load, I had left in Room 16.

The ride home was peaceful. Lainey offered her beloved blanket to cover Nella, and I could see the beginnings of a sister bond forming. Brett played Bob Marley on the radio, and we talked about what we wanted to do that night once we had settled in. My mom was waiting for us and had apparently cleaned the entire house, Gary had a pot of spaghetti sauce simmering, and my dad had bought a few movies that were ready to roll that night. It was sunny outside and the blue skies and fluttering palm tree fronds were all a part of the underlying truth . . . *Life will move on.*

When we pulled into the driveway, Brett gave a little honk—a ceremonious signal for our triumph of landing home. Pink balloons danced in the breeze and a giant stork stood tall in the grass. "Welcome Home, Nella Cordelia," it said.

Yes, the woman was right . . . *You are so very, very lucky.*

new life

LIGHTNING MIGHT NOT STRIKE THE SAME PLACE twice, but luck sure did in our life, as two and a half years before we welcomed Nella, it was our first girl who made us very, very lucky. Lainey Love was born early in the evening on a warm May night, after twenty-two hours of labor, a little bit of cursing, a lot of moaning, and an anesthesiologist with whom I almost made out when he slid a needle in my back that tingled and cooled and magically made it all go away. Her birth was transforming. At the first sight of her outstretched arms, flailing and grasping; the first touch of her pink skin and inhaled breaths of her newness; the first sounds of her sweet cries and whimpers and comforted grunts when I calmed her and snuggled her into my neck while she was still connected to me, blood covered and naked—I evolved into something new. A mother.

Mothers have multiple hearts—one that beats inside them, rhythmically pumping blood up and down, in and out—and one for every child she welcomes. And while the former of these hearts is brilliantly attached to the body with a labyrinth of nerve connectors that tell it how and when to respond, the latter of these hearts is likewise connected. Your child's sorrows are magnified within you, and you celebrate their joys tenfold. And I felt that the moment Lainey was born. I felt myself grow another heart, one that throbbed within me long after the cord was cut.

Becoming a mother is an adjustment, to say the least. First, there's the merger. You know, Old Life and New Life, two equally important entities that are forced to find a way to live peaceably together once a baby has arrived. For the nine months of pregnancy, the contract of the merger is held up in legal. Negotiations are made between Old and New regarding what each is willing to surrender. A standard contract looks a little something like this:

> On the closing and subject to the provisions of this agreement, Old Life shall merge with and into New Life in accordance with the Parenthood Statutes of Humankind. Upon consummation of the merger (birth of first child), Old Life and New Life shall, subject to applicable laws and this agreement, cease to have certain rights, which include as follows: the right to a clean and orderly house; the right to a quiet house; the right to consume an unlimited amount of alcoholic beverages in one night; the right to store cleaning products in an unlocked cabinet; the right to expect boobs to maintain their form without the support of a padded underwire bra; the right to wander into the bathroom at night without tripping on a toy, losing a toenail, and screaming obscenities; the right to slide your butt into a hot pair of jeans without needing a shoehorn to stuff it in; the right to dip your chicken into flaming hot buffalo sauce without worrying how the milk transfer might upset the baby's stomach; the right to share intimate moments without children, dogs, or flying Polly Pocket dolls interrupting; the right to watch a full hour of television without surrendering to cries for "Dora the Explorer"; the right to not look like an idiot while eliciting a smile for a family photo;

the right to skinny-dip drunk in the middle of the night at the neighbors' house.

Which brings me to the Naked Swan Dive Incident of 2006. Old Life must have known something was coming . . . and it was going to fight like hell for one last hoorah.

IT WAS JULY. BRETT AND I HAD BEEN MARRIED FOR ALL of two weeks, and though the honeymoon was technically over, we subconsciously dealt with the drastic postwedding decrescendo of party planning and celebrating by creating our own opportunities to party when we could. Minireceptions, I called them, a gathering of friends and brown bottles and somewhere, deep within, the muffled cries of Old Life. "Keep going! Party on! Please, don't let it be over!" And we listened, drinking Life in grand gulps while the Old Life tap was still flowing freely.

Matt and Dede live across the street from us. Their house has the same floor plan as ours except their tile isn't fifteen years old, their baseboards aren't scuffed and paint chipped, and their kitchen looks like something from *Home & Design* magazine. Dede is the "hostess with the mostest," and even if we're headed out for dinner at a restaurant together, the night always commences with appetizers and drinks in Dede's kitchen. And by appetizers and drinks, I don't mean cheese balls and Corona cans. No, appetizers at Dede's means some special cracker crowned with fresh salmon and capers and little bits of chopped egg that are served with Tiffany hors d'oeuvres forks and Baccarat champagne flutes, perfectly poured and presented with silver *M&D* monogrammed cocktail napkins. Yeah. That's how they roll—a far cry from the paper Party City plates that grace my kitchen.

And so the night started there—in their candlelit kitchen with the brilliant black granite where *Bottle of Champagne Numero Uno* was poured, later to be followed by Uno's friends Quatro, Cinco, and their wild-child sister, Seis. After Round One and our fair share of salmon-

heaped crackers, we took our Wine & Dine down to Naples's Fifth Avenue where the four of us sat in plush white couches under crystal chande- liers and sliced filet that cost far too much. We laughed and told stories while Dede and I drank like it was our job.

Hours later, we were back at Matt and Dede's, and I was clearly drunk. There hadn't been many other times in my life I had made it this far. Maybe just that one time I experimented with vanilla vodka and a bag of marshmallows with my cousin Joann. And, if I remember correctly, it was followed by ten minutes of jumping on the bed at my dad's house. That's right—two grown, wasted women having a sleepover at my dad's, and there we were vaulting off the mattress, throwing our hands in the air and giggling like kids. The jumping of course was quickly followed by a trip to the toilet, where I was curled up for the rest of the night curs- ing my stupidity for the marshmallows—and the jumping. Like adding a cup of sugar to a bottle of corn syrup before drinking and then asking someone to beat your head with a stick just for kicks. Needless to say, vanilla vodka has been blacklisted from the liquor cabinet ever since.

Apparently, Brett tells me, after the tired phase-out period of drink- ing for me comes a second high—the Rockstar High. It was one in the morning, we were on God-knows-what bottle of champagne (or maybe it's better he didn't know), I was sitting on the couch being loud and ob-noxious when someone joked, "We should go skinny-dipping." Legend has it that I peeled off my clothes so fast there was smoke, and I threw my dress into the air (it landed on Matt's head) and ran like a fox, naked and screaming, into the pool.

"Woo-hoo!" someone shrieked. Or maybe it was me. At this point, it really didn't matter. Three more naked bodies came running. Three more bare asses, silhouetted by the moon. Three more "Woo-hoos." We swam and laughed, and Dede and I practiced our swan dives. Which, when you're drunk, isn't anything too fancy, really—just two grown na-ked women holding hands, running like Seabiscuit, and diving into a pool, screaming. Then the boys would judge our dives, which, based on splash intensity and scream volume, would garner us anywhere be-tween an 8 and 9.5. Somewhere around three o'clock in the morning, it dawned on Brett that the neighbors might think we're crazy.

"What if Brekke or Kathleen comes out to check on the noise?" he asked. Brekke and Kathleen are our neighbors, our second set of par-ents, our responsible sixtysomething couple on this street who invite us in for lemonade and haul our garbage cans up the driveway for us when we forget.

"Dude," Matt answered, "Brekke takes the dog out in his boxers all the time. I don't think he'll care." We laughed, picturing Brekke and Kathleen peeking over the pool screen to see a pile of empty champagne bottles and their four grown neighbors naked, gliding in the moonlit pool. And we decided they'd probably be okay with it. "Those crazy kids are just having fun," they'd say. Or so we hoped.

By four o'clock, I was barely hanging on to Rockstar Kelle. We finally walked home—or, at least, I think we walked. We very well could have cartwheeled, somersaulted—hell, we could have high-kicked a synchro-nized dance to "Rocket Man" for all I know, but we did make it home and it didn't hurt that our house was directly across the street. Based on the fact that I woke up naked the next morning holding my purse and the fact that Dede called to let me know she found my underwear in her kitchen sink, I'm pretty sure I walked home bare-ass clutching noth-

ing more than a purse. A few days later a mutual friend of ours had coffee at Dede's house and alerted her that there was a black bra hanging
over her bougainvillea bush. So, upon the invitation of a skinny-dip that
night, not only did I tear off my dress and fling it, but the bra went flying
too. Moral of the story: Old Life went balls out with its grand finale, and
its trophy stands tall in the Hall of Fame of Old Life memories. Three
weeks later a stick with two pink lines confirmed it: *Move over, Old Life.
New Life's a comin'.*

Thankfully, the last of the merger's negotiations were finalized right
before that blissful May evening when my girl—all six pounds, eight
ounces of her—fit into my longing embrace. And I learned quickly just
how severely life can turn from lighthearted drinking days, throwing
caution to the wind, to taking life very seriously, surrendering to the
protective mama bear instincts that dwell within but lie dormant until life isn't just about you anymore. You see, there's fine print in that
merger—fine print that doesn't really do any good to read anyway because you don't believe it until you feel it. The fine print not only warns
you of your joy receptors being stimulated to immeasurable propor-
tions, but it warns you of the pain—the searing pain that loving a child
brings—pain that sometimes seems unbearable, like a knife that's been
stabbed and twisted inside you. I tasted it just days after my firstborn
was placed in my arms.

I had heard stories about jaundice—had watched enough TLC's *A
Baby Story* to know it's no big deal. That a couple days after your baby is
born, she gets pricked in the heel by some lab tech who doesn't seem to
know what she's doing, and you tell her to hurry while she's squeezing
the bejesus out of your little one's foot. And as soon as she caps the blood
tube and tapes a cotton ball on the bloody dot, you protectively swoop
in to scoop up your crying one and hush her softly while you shoot the
stink-eye to the woman who seems to think it's no big deal that the thing
you just fell madly in love with is upset because of her. I knew this. And
yet I didn't know that jaundice can also be bigger than no-big-deal. I
didn't know that there are two kinds of bilirubin, and that when they're

escalating to dangerous levels and not responding to blue light the way they should, doctors start to worry. And they order more tests, which mean more lab techs and more screaming and more stink-eyes. And when the results of those tests don't offer any answers, they call in specialists and send you in an ambulance to a different hospital with your tiny little newborn strapped to a big stretcher. And they tell you all sorts of things it could be. Like *biliary atresia*. And when you press the doctor for worst-case scenario because you're *that* kind of new mom, you might hear things like "liver transplant." And the searing pain part that appears in tiny print in the disclaimer at the bottom of *The Merger of Old Life and New Life*? Yeah, you feel it.

Loving a child hurts so good and so bad at the same time. And, in the middle of the night on Day Four after my Lainey was born, I went there. To that place. I looked at my friend Jen and could barely breathe the words. "Jen, what if she dies?" Because I had to say it. Because I needed someone who was also a mama to tell me that she gets it. That I'm not crazy for loving like this—for feeling like I would surely die too if this heart I grew stopped beating. The same heart whose little liver started working perfectly six days later. After ten days of tests and waiting and bracing ourselves for the worst, a GI specialist diagnosed our little nightmare as nothing more than some blocked liver ducts that began clearing themselves on their own. And my little tanned-skin cub came home as we began to drink in all the joys she would bring.

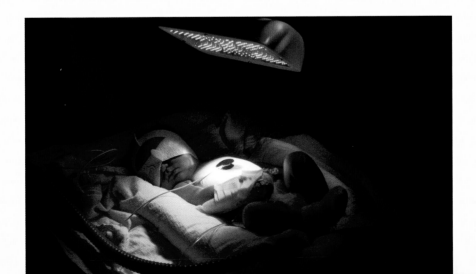

By the time we finally made it home for good and I could relax and settle into New Life comfortably and beautifully, it was all just *so good.* I had heard stories of moms who freak out once they're home from the hospital and think that they can't do it on their own, and while I knew this was a possibility and have no judgments on any mama who has faced a breakdown once home (believe me, I understand, and I have been there along the way), everything came strangely naturally to me those first days at home. I knew what to do when Lainey cried. I knew how to hold her, how to feed her, how to bathe her. I spent hours staring at her tiny features and felt like I constantly had to pinch myself that, yes, this dreamy perfect world of loving a child was real. Her breath was my oxygen. And I couldn't get enough.

I don't think it ever stops being surreal when you become a mother. It's just this constant state of *I can't believe I have a baby, I can't believe I have a two-year-old, I can't believe I have a kindergartener, I can't believe I have a teenager,* and then one day you wake up, hopefully not sooner than later, and ask yourself, *When the hell did I become a grandma?* For me, I had looked forward to being a mother for so long. I mean, for crying out loud, I had all those fake kids' pictures in my childhood purse and now that it was real, it almost felt like I was playing house. Like *Groundhog Day* except instead of waking up to sleet in Punxsutawney, it was Christmas morning every single day. Don't get me wrong, there are days that feel more like Christmas cleanup when there's nothing but a heaping mess of shredded wrapping paper, and I've had those days. At three months old, Lainey boycotted naps completely for two whole weeks to the point where if she slept for ten minutes in the car, we actually did a victory dance. And, despite the fact that I loved breastfeeding and found it a magically bonding and spiritual time, my milk slowly dwindled against my will. Finally, four months, a bottle of fenugreek pills, and two boxes of nursing tea into it, I sat on the floor one night crying with a breast pump attached on high speed, full suction (which, for those who haven't felt it, is like a Hoover vac on crack) for forty-five minutes until, sore boobed and sobbing, I looked down to the empty bottles and proclaimed the battle was over and I sadly had lost. I practically lost my mind trying to figure out why she cried every night at six months until I realized that babies grow teeth then, and growing teeth hurts. Yes, there were trying times when I questioned myself as a mom or didn't have the answers or felt completely exhausted at the end of the night. But the good *always* outweighed the bad to the point of trampling it to nonexistence.

I remember one night in particular. Lainey was five months old. It was Halloween and I had spent the evening doing all the things I had dreamed of my entire life. Dressing up my little girl in a teddy bear costume. Painting a glossy black nose right between her cherub cheeks. Hauling her around our neighborhood in a red Radio Flyer wagon and smiling as neighbors gushed over her cuteness. Later, after her brothers pillaged her candy and we washed the face paint off, after a bath and the prebed ritual of Burt's Bees buttermilk baby lotion and reading *Goodnight Moon*, after prayers and kisses and whispering into her ear how rich she made my life, I looked over at Brett whose smile could barely be seen in the moonlight—the same moonlight that had, a year earlier, glowed upon four bare asses as they swam in the pool across the street. And now, here we were, Lainey snuggled between us, and it was so perfect, I started to cry.

"I'm so happy," I whispered. "I can't believe how incredible it is to have a child. Tonight was so much fun, Brett. For all the times I trick-or-treated as a kid and waited like crazy for Halloween to arrive—and, I'm talkin' I have some *great* Halloween memories—but, seriously? I've never enjoyed it as much as I did tonight."

Brett smiled. He, of course, knew this joy long before me. And for all the times I may have felt a little sting when he had to cancel our romantic plans for parenting-related reasons back in the dating days, and for all his explanations of "you just wait," I finally got it. He was right. There really is nothing like it. And as he wrapped one arm around our little teddy bear that night and stretched the other one out to grab my hand, he had only one thing to say: "I told you so."

BY THE TIME LAINEY WAS SEVEN MONTHS OLD, WE hadn't even hit the first birthday mark and I was already lamenting how fast time flew. I cried when I traded in the 3-to-6-month sleepers for the 6-to-9-month ones, when she hit another milestone, when she could no longer fit into the bassinet beside our bed without her little feet hanging out. Everything was just so . . . *memorable.* I began to feel like I was cupping my hands, attempting to hold water when it just trickled through my fingers and there was nothing I could do to keep it there. I wanted to remember everything. My mom has always talked about dreams she'll have to this day—dreams where we're little again and she's pushing strollers and rocking babies. She says when she wakes up and realizes it's not true—that those days are gone and we're all grown up—that, for a minute, she feels like she can't breathe. Because she wants to feel it again so badly, to hold our little bodies and rock them close to her chest just one more time.

Right before Lainey's first Christmas, I decided to start a blog. My sister had recently started one and so had a couple of my friends, and it seemed like a great way to preserve the present—not to mention a fantastic creative outlet for me as my photography skills were budding and my journaling had dwindled to an occasional entry I wrote in my tattered diary before bed. When I really started getting into photography—shortly before Lainey was born—it was life changing for me. I tapped into new creative energy I didn't realize I possessed, and clicking the shutter of my camera to capture a great shot not only gave me just that—a great shot—but it changed the way I looked at things. I began to notice more when the sky was unusually vivid, when light trickled perfectly through branches to cast golden shadows, when a look on my baby's face was one I hadn't seen before. And composing a memorable image made me appreciate a bit more the emotion and meaning of that moment. Now that Lainey was here, there was so much more I wanted to do. I needed an outlet beyond photography, and the blog was a great way to combine everything. I wanted my kids to be able to know me as a mom of little ones someday. I imagined them reading my stories years later with their own little on their knee and finally getting it—how much I loved them. How full my heart was. My blog would be a legacy, I decided, my own virtual creative diary, a place for me to put it all out there. Photos of my girl, ramblings of my heart, details of every little thing I loved about life. I wanted it to be more than just a scrapbook—I wanted it to be a place full of meaning and beauty, for myself and for my family. When I created the blog late that December night, I was prompted for a title. I thought for a moment, typed in "enjoyingthesmallthings," clicked to submit it, and waited while Blogger searched to see if the URL was available.

"URL Available" popped up in tiny green print a moment later, and I clicked the red "Create Blog" button, making it official. My first entry included these words: *So, here it is . . . a blank page. My hands are shaking! I can't wait to fill it . . . with the little things that make me happy.* Little did I know how full that space out in the ether would become.

It wasn't long before I had a nice home life and creative life going, blended and beautiful. Intertwined with ordinary days, when we took picnics to the park and enjoyed long baths before bed and more trying ones when Lainey knocked over the oatmeal canister for the third time or I couldn't keep up with the laundry, were nights where I'd settle into my desk chair after Lainey was fast asleep, pour myself a cold beer, and write. I wrote about the moments I wanted to remember—the funny, happy, beautiful things I knew I would otherwise forget.

THURSDAY, APRIL 24, 2008: Why I Love Mornings: It's not about the coffee anymore or the way the sun stretches into our living room. It's not my big white robe or that refreshing feeling that everything is new. Those are good reasons, yes. But, I have new reasons why I love mornings. I love . . . the way she's not ready to give up her blankie yet 'cuz she's still a little sleepy . . . the way her bed head makes me smile . . . the way she goes into her food trance when she's eating her scrambled eggs . . . the way her socks—at least one of them— always find a way of falling off in the night . . . the way her pudgy little fingers shove breakfast into her mouth. Mornings are so delicious now.

WEDNESDAY, JULY 23, 2008: Lainey, every morning, at 7:30, on the monitor beside my bed, I hear you shake the side of your crib. You don't cry. You don't talk . . . you just shake, shake, shake the side railing. And so it is . . . I come to find you standing in the sunlight, blankie in one hand, pacifier in mouth. There

is no dramatic welcome when I come to scoop you in my arms . . . just a twinkle in your eye and upward arms. It is then that I hug you, give you a big happy "Good morning, Sunshine!" and take you out to the couch where we lie, snuggle, and slowly wake up . . . together. And this is the way it goes. I love your sleepy eyes that blink-blink-blink first thing in the morning sunlight that streams in from the front door and lands in a puddle on the couch cushions. The way you quietly suck your pacifier, giving it a rhythm that tugs like a teasing little fish on a bobber at the water's surface. Your first yawn that makes you look like a lion cub. Your not-quite-ready-for-my-day cuddle and the way you lay your head on my tummy and rub the satiny part of my nightgown between your fingers until . . . slowly, you lift your heavy head and welcome your surroundings . . . Good morning, World. And then . . . your first smile of the day.

MONDAY, OCTOBER 6, 2008: Today, we made pumpkin bread, her in her little apron and me in mine. I started by letting her stir and drop in pre-measured teaspoons but realized her independence was craving more. So, I let her have her own bowl filled with a little flour and some spices. For the next half hour, she was in heaven,

stirring, sprinkling, shoveling heaps of flour onto the floor. . . . and I couldn't stop smiling. This kid thing? This having a daughter thing? So. Much. Fun. She's my friend . . . my little buddy, and hanging out with her all day is so incredibly fulfilling. I love her.

Every time I wrote—every time I looked through pictures of our week and strung together the important stories—the little things—and published them on the blog, I walked deeper into Gratitude. My love affair with writing was rekindled, and combined with motherhood and family life and falling into this amazing happiness along with reflecting about it on the blog, I was finding more ways to look at the events in my life as beautiful. It became an art—an art that gave back in so many ways. My family in Michigan began following, Brett's family soon caught on, and it wasn't long before I had a small readership of friends, family, and a few strangers who logged on to follow along.

Shortly after creating the blog, I landed upon the blog of another mom on the other side of the country. Nici lived in Montana, was pregnant with her first baby, and spent her days living out the fantasies of the very cool mom that dwelled in my head. Like, she grew her own food, canned peaches in her kitchen, wrangled chickens in her backyard, and used the word *organic* a lot. Nici was cool. And the more I followed her blog well after the birth of her baby girl, the more I realized that despite the fact that we were very different, we were very much the same indeed. We both loved to write, we loved our girls something fierce, we dabbled in a handful of elective creative endeavors, and we shared an insatiable appetite for life.

Soon we were e-mailing, texting, talking on the phone. Our girls would sit on our laps while we Skype-chatted and traded stories of new opportunities and dreaming of more babies. Strangely, our lives paralleled each other regardless of the fact that I had never blanched peas and wouldn't know a canning jar if it hit me in the face. But still, a friendship grew. To the point that we were dying to meet each other and so we teased that someday it would happen and that our girls would be slung to our hips while we ran, slow motion, through a field of daisies, open armed, with the *Chariots of Fire* theme song playing . . . right to each other where we would hug long and say things like "you look different in real life." The thing is, blogging not only created a place for me to put it all down—the memories, the love, the little moments I wanted my kids to know about—but it connected me to different worlds where a strong commonality dwelled . . . that there are many out there doing this—this "searching for the good and drinking in the moment" thing.

Motherhood brought everything I dreamed it would, and yet so much more. And while, yes, Old Life may have folded up its nights of champagne and skinny-dipping and put them far away, New Life matched its excitement in different new ways. New Life too had a Hall of Fame that was quickly filling with its own trophies—trophies that not only stood tall in our memories but that were preserved in writing and photos and stories of just how good our life really was. I didn't think it could get much better, but then again, I didn't know that fate had a sweet little thing lined up . . . a sweet little thing named Nella Cordelia.

chapter 7
week one

THERE'S A REASON OPENING WORDS LIKE *CALL ME Ishmael* or *It was the best of times; it was the worst of times* are seared into our minds, and I was hell-bent on making sure the first words in our new narrative were poignantly comparable. I remember unbuckling Nella from her car seat once the car had stopped, scooping up her tiny body, and securing it in the nook of my left arm, heading toward the door, past the balloons and stork signs, and actually visualizing the very first words of an epic masterpiece being scribbled on virgin paper. *This is the beginning of our story,* I whispered in my head, *and it's going to be beautiful.* I smiled. The sun was shining and Lainey was excitedly telling us her plans for the rest of the day. Like we would play with dolls and maybe make cupcakes and she would push "Baby 'Ella" in the pink stroller later for a walk around the neighborhood.

When you're an adult, you learn to figure things out on your own. Gone are the days when you are seven and you attempt to walk across the monkey bars like your brother and you slip off and land on your back so hard, the wind gets knocked out of you. And though you're sure there's a good chance you'll never walk again, it doesn't matter. It doesn't matter because you know your mom saw you from the kitchen window and in just about two seconds, you're going to hear the back door slam and she's going to come running, calling your name and telling you it's okay. And, no matter what, she'll fix it. Because that's what moms do. When your body is hot and your head is throbbing and you're trying not to cry hunched over your *Weekly Reader* in Mrs. Rizzi's first-grade class because you're sick and you don't want your friends to think you're a baby, when you hear the PA beep in and say, "Mrs. Rizzi, would you please send Kelle down to the office? Her mother is here to pick her up," you know it's all going to be fine. And you know she'll make homemade chicken soup and baby you more than seven-year-olds should be babied. She'll buy you 7Up and Gummi Bears because that's what you like when you're sick. And she'll make it better . . . because she's your mom. When you're all grown up, though, you have to pick *yourself* up off the ground and make it better because you're an adult and adults have to fix things themselves. But sometimes there are exceptions. Sometimes, you get a *Get-Out-of-Adulthood-Free* card and you can, for a moment, wave your card and wait for your mom to come running. And she'll help you fix it.

When I walked into the door of our home that day holding my new baby in my arms, emotionally drained, physically exhausted, smiling but likely to fall to my knees in a catastrophic breakdown at any given moment, my mom was there waiting. Standing in my kitchen, smiling, ready to scoop Nella out of my arms and smother her with kisses—the Grandma Krissy kind that are loud, drawn-out smooches. Smooches on the cheek, on the neck, on the top of her head, and the sound of lips-to-skin that can be heard from across the street.

My mother is the epitome of maternal. She crochets hats and booties and intricate coming-home-from-the-hospital ensembles for all the grandkids. She can make award-winning casseroles from the most hodgepodge collection of pantry staples. She knows how to get baby puke stains out of white cotton and can cut up an old curtain and transform it into a set of elegant dinner napkins embroidered with our names. And, every year, for Christmas, she wins what my family has deemed the Jesse Bear Award. The Jesse Bear Award was named after some clearance bear she found for one of the kids years ago who, upon opening it, ditched all the other lovely gifts we had purchased and proclaimed their Christmas love for Jesse and Jesse alone. Hence the Jesse Bear Award—the "favorite gift" award, and she has it in the bag every year.

My mom is the queen of baby talk. When a baby cries, Mom holds her arms out and does this whole "Oh, does you needs Grammas? Whadda matter, Babykins? You come see Grammas" thing. And then she swoops them away, huddling them close, mumbling, rocking, and bouncing until Baby goes into a grandma trance of tranquility and comfort.

The day we came home was no different. No sooner had we walked in the door than Nella was scooped and swooped and kissed and comforted with "Oh, just wook at dat pwetty baby!" And as my mom walked away with her, I stopped and looked around at my house. It was all the same. While it felt like my old life had withered and died, nothing had changed here. There were piles of clean laundry my mom had folded, a pot of spaghetti sauce simmering on the stove, Lainey's toys scattered around the playroom, stacks of unopened mail on the counter, and enough of a controlled mess to keep me from becoming overwhelmed while at the same time comforting me with a sense of normalcy. Lord knows Mess equals Normal at our home, and if it were too clean, it would have reminded me that things were indeed very different from how they were just a few days ago.

A small decorative chalkboard stood on an easel on the island in the kitchen. I glanced down to see what I had so carefully scripted with white chalk just moments before we had walked out the door to head to the hospital. "Welcome Home, Nella! We Love You!" it read. The last letter of each word scrolled into an elaborate curl, and there was an outline of a flowering vine I had doodled along the edge of the slate. For a moment, it stung. I thought about the woman who had written that. Who had excitedly spent the time to doodle flowers and a message to

the baby she was about to meet. It was *Me*. Before this all happened. I thought about her like she was a different person, someone I used to know—someone I used to be—and I wondered if she would come back or if she was lost forever like a face on a milk carton, frozen in time. For a moment, I wanted to cry again—to heave my body onto the island countertop and expel again the agony of the shock and what it meant. And, at the same time, it felt a bit silly. Overly dramatic when everything at this very moment was fine, normal—perhaps even happy.

A baby had just been born. A baby had just been welcomed into the world where waiting hearts now celebrated. Grandparents doted. Cards and flowers filled the car, and texts flew in like air traffic control alerts. I can never stress enough the propelling power that celebration of life had on me. I needed it like oxygen. While I dealt with my grief and tried to figure out how the hell we were going to do this, I needed the catalyst of positivity to push me forward, and it came with every "Congratulations on that beautiful baby!" With warm, genuine smiles. With listening to friends shout "Dibs on Nella first!" when they walked in the door, threw their purses to the ground, and strong-armed each other to get to her. Like no one was listening when they first said she had Down syndrome.

When Lainey was born and I took her home from the hospital, my mom helped me give her the first bath. I wanted the tradition to continue and so, shortly after we arrived home, I proclaimed it time for Nella's very first bath and gathered sweet soaps and lotions and a soft sleeper to slip her into once she was clean. My dad had suggested Lainey take a bath with Nella to make it more memorable and encourage some bonding, so the hubbub of preparations for the big to-do began. The camera, the video camera—it all had to be ready, but there was something else that needed to be done. Something that Daddy insisted upon. I didn't realize how important it was until I found my husband, just an hour or so after bringing our new girl home and prepping for her bath, in the garage by himself. There he stood, ransacking cluttered shelves obviously in search of something. He didn't even notice the door had opened when I walked in but instead stayed focused, pulling things off shelves, peeking in boxes, rearranging the cluttered mess. I looked closer. He was crying. My husband's eyes were red and pooled with tears he had struggled to keep hidden.

"Oh, babe, why are you crying?" My heart ached for him. For all the times he'd held it together these past several days and portrayed such calm assurance, I wondered what it was in this garage that set him off. Brett has never been one to pour his emotions out or find comfort in talking about his sadness like I do and I knew he probably wouldn't expound, but we were in this together and I wanted to do something—*anything*—to fix his broken heart at that moment.

"I'm fine. I'm fine. Just . . ." He trailed off for a moment. "I'm fine." He sucked it in. Dabbed his eyes quickly as if he could hide the fact that he was having a moment.

"Tell me. What? Are you sad? Oh, babe, please tell me. What are you thinking about? What's making you sad? Why are you in the garage and what are you looking for?"

I saw them again, the tears he was working so hard to dam up. He straightened his back and breathed in deeply. "I'm looking for the space heater," he whispered. "It's her first bath and I don't want her to be cold. She needs a heater."

And that is my husband. A true father. If it's broken and he doesn't know what to do to fix it, to make his kids better, he can love. He can heat up bathrooms for cozy baths. He can roll up blankets to prop droopy heads in the car seat. He can make sure everything is safely installed, that new batteries are in the swing, electrical outlets are covered, crib sheets are washed, and that babies sleep on their backs because that's what the doctor says is safest. And doing these things makes him feel powerful, loving, and protective when he's otherwise at a loss. And although he never really talked a lot about Down syndrome and how it scared him—at least not like I did because that was healing for me—he slowly healed his broken heart by doing. While he couldn't sweep away a syndrome, he could soothe away a chill. He could be the best father he could be. He could dig through old boxes in the garage to find the space heater so he could warm up the bathroom for his little girl's very first bath in her new home.

I'll never forget that first bath—not so much because I was focused on Nella or Lainey or even the fact that I had two daughters in a tub of buttermilk bath suds and that's what I'd always wanted, but because my mom and my dad were both together helping me. Sure, since the divorce we had had a handful of events in our life where they were together—some Christmas Eves, grandkids' birthdays, weddings . . . but this? It was definitely one of those "this is strange" moments, like it was exactly what it would have been like had they never been divorced. We were all together in the intimate space of our master bath, all hunched over the porcelain edge of the tub, reaching down to rinse hair, snap pictures, coo and goo and make sure behind the ears got scrubbed. My mom took care of Nella, my dad oversaw Lainey, and I was left in the middle to make sense of it all. Volleying my glance back from my mom to my dad, from Nella to Lainey, thinking about the fact that everyone was happy and helping and was here at this moment for the purpose of doing what families are supposed to do. Nothing else mattered. I needed them both, and they knew it.

The rest of the day was strangely just as it should be for a baby's first day home—a holiday of sorts. We ate good food and watched a good movie. We stretched out on the couch with afghans draped over us and passed Nella from one person to the next. We even took that walk with Lainey around a couple blocks, drinking in the mild sun and chillier temperatures of a good Florida January. I kept Nella snugly stretched against my chest in the baby sling, hoping no one in the neighborhood would recognize me as the previously big-bellied mama and come running over to see the new baby. Because I wasn't up for the awkward moment where I stood there and watched them smile and say, "Oh, she's beautiful," all the while wondering if they noticed or if I should say something. And what do you say? "Thank you. By the way, she has Down syndrome."

In the hospital, I had a moment where I thought

it would be appropriate to send out troops to tell everyone and their brother that Nella had Down syndrome. The thought of announcing it over and over killed me as much as the repeated awkwardness of bumping into people who hadn't heard. I knew our friends and family would find out immediately, but what about acquaintances? What about the neighbors? What about the girl who cut my hair? During the temporary insane period of my grief, I actually suggested that someone go door-to-door to everyone we knew and tell the neighbors. Which is when my tell-it-like-it-is friend Katie jumped in.

"Let me get this straight," she said. "You want me to go knocking on everyone's door like a freaking Girl Scout and say what? 'Hey, you know the Hamptons? Yeah, the ones with the fountain in the front yard? Yup, well, um, their baby? Down syndrome, man. Down syndrome.'"

At that point, I erupted in laughter, recognizing the ridiculousness of my suggestion.

"You know, Kelle," she continued, "you don't have to say anything. You pull the blanket off her face when people want to see, and you smile and be proud and tell them her name."

"What if they're wondering if she has it?" I asked.

"Then they're wondering if she has it. So what? It doesn't matter."

As true as those words were, I hastened through our walk that day, protectively clutching Nella as close to me as I could get her and taking quick steps back home, away from the open air and the world that seemed so threatening at the time. I just wasn't quite ready to face it,

and I needed the security of our home where my mom was inside baking something sweet. At least for now.

If bringing Nella home started the next chapter in our family's story, having her there with us in our sacred space put me in the headspace of knowing what else I needed to do . . . actually sit down and write about her birth. Since I was little, when something big happens in my life—good or bad—I've run to write about it. Years ago my healing process started in hardback diaries and notebooks where I scribbled things with my four-color pen from the simple and blunt statements like "Today sucked major ass" to more dramatic entries where the soap opera within me was unleashed with words such as "The tears flow like rivers as I write, and the heartache cuts me like a knife." I was sixteen.

Over time, writing about things that weighed on my mind became a sort of therapy—an emotional purging of moments and feelings I needed to get off my chest. Diaries and notebooks gradually turned into folders on my laptop with titles such as "Motherhood" or "Family" or whatever topic I seemed to be waxing on about at the moment. Later, in blog posts, I published random epiphanies and chronicled Lainey's milestones for friends and family. Usually, by the last words of my entry and through the process of thinking about things long enough to put them into a personal essay, I had figured things out a bit more. Closing my laptop after a good writing session became synonymous with getting up off the therapist's couch and thanking her for an hour of her time. Except my pocket got to keep the $115, thank you very much.

I knew writing about Nella's birth would prove to be a very big step toward acceptance and healing, and yet at the same time, I was fully aware that the process of writing it all down would be one of the most painful experiences of my life—that it would hurt like hell to go there and that revisiting those first emotions would rip away the thin skin that had barely begun to cover my wounds and expose raw flesh and bone once again. But writing about it was necessary to my being, and I knew it was perhaps the single most important thing I would ever put fingertips to keys to say, the single most important thing I would ever try to make sense of.

So it was, on the one-week birthday of my girl, I closed myself into the quiet of my bedroom. My mom and Brett held down the fort outside that door while I wrote that evening, knowing the importance of what I was doing and what it meant for the next steps on my journey. And I knew I could not move forward until I had finished the monumental task of putting words to the first moment I held my Nella Cordelia just a week before.

It began with setting the scene. I needed to "feel it" to write it. While emotions seemed dammed up within and I was certain they'd spill forth once my fingers began tapping keys, I needed more. I pulled the curtains closed and flicked the switch to the six flameless candles that were present in the birth room. Their batteries still stood strong, miraculously, after flickering twenty-four hours a day during our hospital stay, and it felt right to have them glowing once again while I wrote about her birth. I wrapped Nella tightly in a gauzy blanket and placed her into a nook on my bed between my pillows, right next to where I would sit and type her story. I wanted to see her—to hear her breathy sleep—while I wrote. Finally, before I began, I heard the door open and Brett walked into the low glow of candlelight holding a beer.

"Here, babe. You might need this." I know I've stressed this point before, but seriously, my husband has a rare gift—an insanely acute radar for knowing just when someone needs a beer, and it is his mission in life to deliver, bringing frosty beers to the needy so the world might be a brighter, happier place. And though I inappropriately mock his kind and beer-loving heart, I thanked him for what it was worth during those moments and took my frosty beer and drank it. Because I'm selfless like that.

I don't know how I knew where to begin or even how long it took me to write the story of my daughter's birth, but I do know that over the course of at least a few hours, I was chained to my bed, where I rhythmically typed nonstop, tears streaming, stomach lurching, feeling the raw throbbing wounds again in that candlelit room. I did not edit, I did not reread, I did not pause to think about how to word it. I simply wrote—seamlessly—and surrendered to the emotional dam breaking, stopping only a few times to scoop Nella into my arms, hold her close, and feel her body against my heaving sobs. "I love you," I whispered to her. "I love you so much."

With each word I wrote, I felt the weight of my sadness and fears literally melting into a healing place. It felt good. It felt freeing. And though it hurt to tap into some of those feelings—the ones I was afraid to say out loud—it was a restoring pain. I needed to let myself know it was okay to feel the way I did, and somehow, by writing it all out, I forgave myself for the parts of me I didn't like, I accepted myself for the parts I was working on, and I loved myself for the part of me that saw beyond all this and knew it was going to come together for good, that life is bigger than what we expect. And more important, digging deep within myself and extracting all the feelings I had toward that life-changing day not only made me appreciate the moments and the people I encountered during it, but it ignited a deeper love for my girl—something not even a birth story could really explain.

On the one-week birthday of Nella Cordelia, I gave birth again—to her story. And hours later that evening, I stopped typing. I had done it. Usually after writing a long piece, I'll go back and edit and rewrite a bit, but I was completely drained. So, without even rereading, I hit "Publish." It was finished. I called my dad from the bedroom. I didn't even say hello when he answered.

"I did it, Dad. I wrote it."

"I'm on my way to my computer right now," he answered. And he hung up.

I scooped Nella up from the bed, turned off my candles, closed the computer, and reemerged from the bedroom, tearstained and tired but feeling a hundred pounds lighter, ready to join my mom and Brett and Lainey for popcorn and a wholesome Hallmark movie my mom had brought with her because she always brings wholesome movies when she comes to stay with us. For the first time in a long time, I felt I could truly relax and let go—that everything would somehow end up okay and that even if it didn't, we'd figure it out. But right then, I thought of nothing else but that moment. That moment when I sat on big pillows in our living room and watched an uplifting movie while my mom crocheted, Lainey climbed on top of me, the boys laughed and played video games in their rooms, and Brett set out in the kitchen to create ice cream sundaes. Nella slept, nestled in the Moses basket amidst all of us, and between indulging in heaping spoonfuls of chocolate-drizzled vanilla and snuggling with Lainey, who was happy to have her mama finally fully present, I glanced occasionally at Nella and swallowed a small taste of victory. I had told her story.

Unbeknownst to me at that moment, Nella's birth story would travel. Slowly at first, to family and friends, and then soon to friends of friends . . . and friends of their friends. Overnight, comments poured in—beautiful, touching words that healed my hurting heart, but I still had no idea of the magnitude of how her story would spread. A week after I had published it on my blog, I woke up one morning to a phone call from my dad.

"Have you seen the comments on the birth story this morning?" he asked.

After waking up three times in the night to nurse a baby, I hadn't even made coffee yet, forget taking a moment to look at comments—the thought had not crossed my tired mind.

"No, why?"

"Kelle, there are 753 comments."

"What?!" I ran to my computer, clicked into my birth story post, and scrolled down, comment after comment. He was right. There were pages and pages—kind words from beautiful strangers from all over the world.

My dad was crying, beginning to read comments over the phone. And this was just the beginning.

I'VE NEVER BEEN A CYNICAL PERSON, BUT I WOULDN'T necessarily say I've primarily looked for the good in people. I haven't always given people the benefit of the doubt. I've been affected by media that sometimes portray the world as a scary or negative place to be. And I have always been one to stay close to my circle of people I trust, perhaps skeptical of those who exist outside of it. But if there's one thing I learned through those days of opening my computer to find more healing words from strangers, it's that there is so much good in the world. There are so many amazing people who are striving to see beauty, who take time to help a stranger, who challenge themselves to be better—to learn more about people and differences and how to bring them all together. And it turns out that writing the story of Nella's birth not only brought much-needed healing to my heart but perhaps even just as important, it brought humility and the recognition that I am one of millions of human beings who experience pain and ultimately grow because of it. That recognition alone simultaneously comforted and fueled me. Things were slowly shifting as my perspective tilted toward seeing my child having Down syndrome less as an obstacle and more as an opportunity. An opportunity to bloom where we are planted. And if that was the beginning of my story, then this was going to be one hell of a good one.

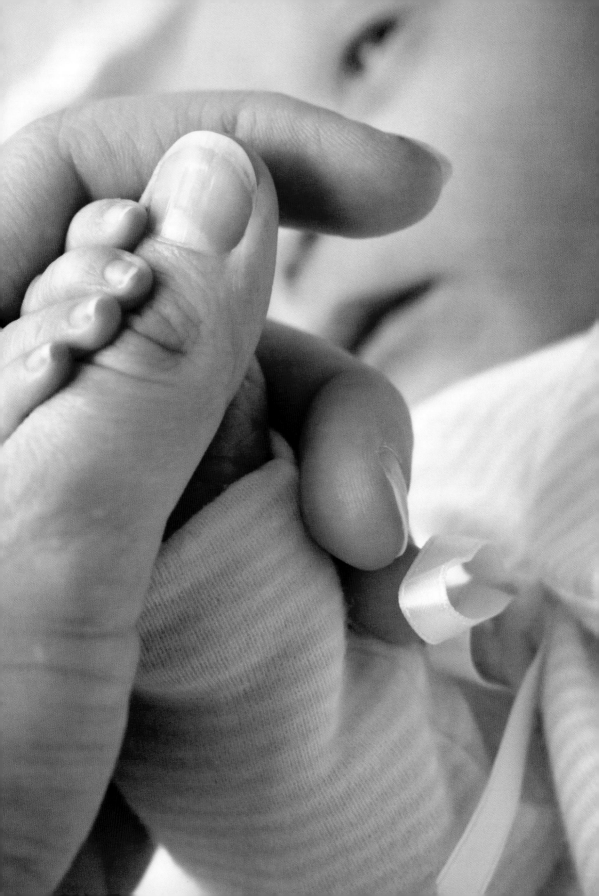

moving on

SEEING THE GOOD IN OTHERS PROPELLED AND
fueled me, but still . . . moving on is hard. Especially when the
training wheels of support—the people at your bedside, holding
your hand, wiping your tears, hugging you tight—are removed.
When the flags of grief are finally raised from half-staff back to
their position, life must move on, even when you want it to stand
still. And while the five days we spent in the hospital held the
most pure and painful grief I've ever experienced, they came
with the emotional padding of a twenty-four-hour support system, of not having to get out of bed to take care of a two-year-old,
of nurses just a small red call button away to bring me drugs to
make it all go away if I needed.

And, as all good learning-to-ride-a-bike experiences go,
pedaling independently those first weeks home with our new
family was a gradual process for me, one where I gripped the
handlebars of life with white knuckles, looking behind me,
around me, pleading with the hands that pushed me along,
"Please, don't let go. I'm not ready yet." Soon, it was time for my

mom to kiss the babies good-bye and return to her home, and while preparing for her absence was unpleasant to say the least, it was the anticipation of another absence that gripped me with the stomach-lurching anxiety of a turbulent flight.

Brett's sales job was requiring him to leave for an indefinite period of time, and by leave I don't mean a road trip up the coast. He was headed to Rockford, Illinois—away from our family and the bit of comfort we were beginning to rebuild, and into the dead gray cold of a midwestern winter where he would spend his time in a cubicle at the office headquarters of his company attending meetings, making sales calls, and staring at his new photo of the four kids he taped next to his computer. I had forgotten to pack a photo in his suitcase and on Day Two away from us, I received a text from him that said simply, *Send photo of my kids NOW. I need it.*

I didn't realize how much I needed him until I pulled away from the airport after dropping him off—two car seats behind me visible from the rearview mirror. Nella was just a day or so shy of two weeks old, I was barely learning how to ride this bike, and my husband—the only one who truly knew how I felt—was being pulled away from our family. And as the tears streamed down my cheeks that day, wondering when I'd see him next and driving off back home as the new mother of two and recovering grief victim, I not only felt like the training wheels and guiding hands of my bike had been ripped away, but that I was being purposefully knocked down.

Up to this point, the grief support Brett and I had provided for each other was an intricate balance, fortunately fated so that both of us were never sad at the same time—like a perfect game of Rock, Paper, Scissors where someone always wins. Rock and Paper. Paper and Scissors. Scissors and Rock. It was as if something in our bodies knew and sensed when the other was falling and adjusted itself accordingly, armed with strength and as many "It's gonna be okay"s necessary to fix the other's despair. The fact that this balance was so naturally orchestrated was, I suppose, the universe's way of throwing us a bone. But, without Brett home and present to sense and adjust my sadness, I felt incredibly vulnerable and alone. My cousin Joann was deployed from Michigan to be by my side, and the loneliness of the days between Brett's departure and her arrival were alleviated by Heidi spending the night, trying to make me laugh, holding Nella, playing with Lainey, and filling in the gaps where I was lacking.

I whined like a two-year-old about Brett having to be gone—cried for two days and took my sadness out on everyone associated with his job as if having someone to blame would make our problems better. In my grief and selfishness, I suppose I expected the universe to stop—that the economy would suddenly take a swing for the good and that Brett's job and the rest of the world would stop and cater to us. Life's a bitch, though. And perhaps that's just another of the trillion lessons I learned through this. There are women who go through far worse—who lose children and have to get up the next day and go to work because there are more mouths to feed and there are bosses who don't care. I had a loving husband who had a good job in a trying economy, and regardless of how many miles separated us, I knew I needed to be thankful and to stop expecting the world to cave in to our needs.

Brett was gone for seventeen days, the longest stretch of time we've ever been apart and definitely the most trying for Lainey, who asked for him every single day. And as much as friends sympathized with me when they heard I was managing a new baby, a two-year-old, and this giant ball of posttraumatic stress on my own, it was actually a good experience for me, like boot camp is good for forcing a young soldier to unlock all the hidden strengths within him. At the close of every day, after the tears and midnight feedings and cleaning up after a toddler and telling her how many more days until her daddy came home; after shedding a little more sadness and grasping a little more acceptance on my own, without the assurance of Brett's presence, I proved to myself just how strong I was. And I was far stronger than I ever knew. Surviving seventeen days as a single mama of two, still half grieving/half greeting, became a minuscule version of the grander picture—and I was making it. I could do this.

My cousin Joann—the same cousin who jumped on the bed with me back in the day when I thought vanilla vodka and a bag of marshmallows complemented each other—had booked her ticket to come be with me just a few days after Nella was born. Joann's not really my cousin. She's married to my cousin, but Cryderman blood runs thick and when you marry a Cryderman, you, by default, inherit all Cryderman qualities, including but not limited to a compassionate sensitivity that can move you from laughter to tears in six seconds flat, a self-deprecating sense of humor, and the innate ability to shove crap into drawers and closets ten minutes before company arrives to fake a clean house. Joann heard my girl's first cries because my dad, in a moment of brilliance and

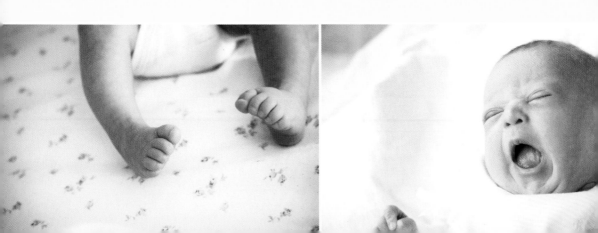

glory, thought to call her from his cell phone in the delivery room right before that last push. And although that call ended with happy tears and a promise from my dad that he'd call back with her birth stats, the call that followed wasn't as happy as she had expected. When my dad told her that Nella had Down syndrome and that she needed to get word out to the family as soon as possible, Joann says she left the high school basketball game she was attending, drove home, told her husband she didn't want to talk about it, and climbed into the shower where she sat down and cried until no tears were left. You see, that's another Cryderman quality. We cry. We wear each other's pains as our own and when there is sorrow, we cry like it's an Olympic sport. "I have to get to her," Joann said. "I have to get to her now." So a ticket was bought and Joann arranged to arrive appropriately while Brett was away.

It's a twenty-two-minute drive from our house to the airport. I know this well because I've driven it a thousand times to pick up loved ones in to visit, and usually the drive there has me in the anticipatory mind-set of a kid on her way to Disney World when two more miles seem like ten and the mirage of the Magic Kingdom seems so close you can see it twinkling. It was an unusually chilly January for Naples and as I cruised along Interstate 75 at a steady seventy-three miles per hour—three more than the required speed limit, maintaining safety and yet giving me the advantage of possibly arriving thirty blessed seconds sooner—I felt my throat tightening and my stomach doing that whole lurching maneuver it had mastered these last weeks.

As I pulled up into the arriving flights lane, I saw Joann's familiar small frame standing near the edge of the curb. Her brown hair, shorter than the last time I had seen her, was neatly tucked behind her ears and she smiled anxiously, waving me down.

"Baby, look! It's Joann." I looked back at Lainey who sat quietly in her car seat, one hand protectively stretched over Nella's seat and resting on her sleeping sister. I made as many conscious efforts as I could these days to talk to her and include her, to let her know I loved her, to reconcile the growing wounds of guilt I had for changing her perfect little world in so many ways in a few short weeks. And the sweeter she responded and the quieter she was—the precious resilience she demonstrated with every smile and kiss and "It's okay, Mama" while she wiped my tears—almost made it harder for me. Perhaps loving her wouldn't hurt so bad if she pitched more fits or maybe threw a book or two at her new sister. But she simply swam with the currents of change with grace and beauty far past her age. I was terrified though that her spirits would sink in the chaos of our new world. What if she feels left out? What if she thinks all these people are visiting just to see Nella and consequently feels inferior? What if inside that little blond head, she's sad or confused or thinking she did something wrong? So I covered when I could, and today, I was two steps ahead in my brilliant plan of telling her Joann came just to see her. Because she heard Lainey had just become a big sister and not just that but the *best* big sister ever and, well, that deserved a special visit from Aunt Joann. "Look, Lainey! Joann's here! She flew on an airplane just like Daddy because she wants to give the best big sister ever a hug!"

I felt like a good mom for the moment, which assuaged my guilt for having her daddy away, for suddenly halving the attention she received, for feeling shitty that morning when I lied and told her the chocolate frosting on the donut she wanted was poop so she wouldn't throw a fit when I said she couldn't have it. For the time being, my firstborn's sweet face was smiling and proud, pleased to have Aunt Joann coming just to see her.

I guided my Jeep along the edge of the pickup curb and shifted it into park, all the while watching Joann and anticipating the hug we would share in just seconds. And then, like long-lost friends, we walked toward each other—slowly at first—closer, closer—until finally we were running those last steps and we embraced so tightly, I could smell her perfume and feel her heaving sobs against my shoulders. We didn't let go. We just stood there, arms locked, bodies shaking, holding each other on the curb while my babies looked through tinted glass from the car window and strangers watched and must have speculated that someone had died or returned from war or maybe finally showed up after something life changing had happened. I pressed my cheek against Joann's and felt the tears that were streaming down her cheeks.

"I love you," she repeated over and over. "I love you so much." It wasn't a sad hug. It wasn't even a pity hug. It was purely a love hug, one that told me she knew everything would be okay and that Nella was perfect and that the only thing she was sorry about was that I had to ride through this middle ground of figuring it all out, and that's hard. We stayed like that for at least a minute while I imagined her body transferring strength into mine for as long as we had contact. When we finally peeled apart, we laughed at how our faces were a hot mess—blotchy and tearstained—and then we threw suitcases into the trunk and climbed into the car where I heard Joann squeal, "Lainey! I couldn't wait to get to you!" while she dug through her purse for presents to hand out. It felt like old times and because of that, it served as another reminder that things didn't have to change as much as I thought they would. Maybe this whole thing was another sort of Old Life/New Life Merger, and maybe we could tear the whole damn thing up and make our own rules. And they would begin with *Old Life resumes the right to relinquish airport pickups and welcoming loved ones and bringing them home for weeks of late-night movies and drinks and morning talks over coffee*. It would follow with rules for continuing all the things we love—dancing silly with our kids in the living room and family walks late at night and gathering with friends for barbecues while we gush about whose kids are growing up too fast and what funny thing our youngest said. And if we still have these things, does it really matter if we also have therapy and more doctor appointments? Is it a tragic loss if Nella doesn't talk like other kids or graduate with honors if she can still grin like the Cheshire cat when aunts and cousins come in from out of town and tell her they couldn't wait to get to her?

I think this is a good place to admit just how much I thought would change when Nella was born. It's silly now, really, to think that I actually had to self-talk myself into the understanding that having a child with Down syndrome didn't mean I'd have to give up welcoming family from the airport or silly dancing to *Kidz Bop* in the living room. I think it's ridiculous that I thought I had to start from scratch—that I let my life crumble in my head because, for years, I had bought in to the cockamamie ideas and standards of young families. A week before she was born, I had used a gift certificate my friends had pooled together to buy an over-the-top pink silk baby book that I paid extra to have "Nella Cordelia" elegantly embroidered across the top. And, I am sorry to say, I had a moment of disappointment after my sweet girl entered the world in which I actually thought, *I guess I can't use that baby book anymore.* I am ashamed to admit that, for a moment, I felt I had used up a beautiful name on a baby I hadn't intended to be the recipient or that I suddenly didn't want to send out a birth announcement when weeks earlier I obsessed over a flat or folded card. This saddens me now. But it was in this beautiful mess of my former self that true potential dwelled—potential to be molded and shaped by a grand defining moment. And when there is potential . . . *there is greatness.*

It's incredibly disappointing when our reality contradicts our ideals, but the challenge and beauty of growing older is realizing that when our ideals embrace what's really important in life, our ideals and reality can dwell harmoniously more often than not. Because ideally, I simply want to see good and do good and find good and, in doing so, I want to be happy and I want my family to be happy. And reality? Well, when adver-

sity strikes in whatever mask it's wearing, it brings with it a greater passion and greater tools to do just that . . . to find good. To see good. To do good. I may not have understood this yet the afternoon I picked up Joann and drove her home with me, but I at least was beginning to open myself up for change. And though it didn't come right away, what did come was a healing week with my cousin where we huddled with the girls like it was Christmas morning.

"Firewood," I said, suddenly remembering, five minutes from home. "We need firewood, Joann, if we're gonna do this week right." *Batten down the hatches* is what I had in mind, as if moving on in the world was equivalent with facing a raging storm and, as all good battening of hatches goes, things seemed easier—cozier perhaps—if they were accompanied by a crackling fire. I imagined us corralled up among cushions and quilts holding babies, watching movies, sipping hot drinks, and letting the unseasonably chilly Florida weather give us an excuse to vacation indoors. I pulled into Target and stopped the car as if our lives depended on a package of Duraflames from aisle 7.

"Oh, thank God you stopped. I didn't think I was going to be able to wait another minute before I got a chance to hold that baby." Joann leaped from her seat and reached back to unleash Nella from her car seat

straps while I unbuckled Lainey and kissed her cheek and whispered "I love you" one more time—another attempt to stash-pile some love for her. Joann pulled Nella out of her seat and held her close to her face, smiling and kissing the top of her head.

"Oh, Kelle, I love her," she whispered as she positioned her gently into the crook of her arm so that Nella was fully visible to the outside world. Joann looked proud. "I hope people think she's mine," she said.

Wow. So that's how it's supposed to be done. No shame. No apologizing. No fumbling for a blanket to cover her because you're not yet ready to wonder what people are thinking or if you should say anything or, for God's sake, have that moment in the grocery store where it just seems unfair. Joann carried Nella proudly as a two-week-old baby girl who was worthy of much praise and, for a moment, I felt ashamed of myself for my previous trip here to this very same place a week earlier.

It was my first journey out. My dad had come with me to grab a few groceries and, although I didn't cry or have a panicked moment of *how-does-one-do-this?* I cautiously tread into the whole going-out-in-public thing, slipping my new girl into the "crutch" of the protective sling that cradled her close to my chest, close to my pain and love, and as far away from the world as I could get her. It wasn't so much that I wanted to cover her as I wanted to cover myself. I was apprehensive. I didn't want people looking, feeling sorry for me. So I entered the store smiling and pretended I was just like any other new mom. And it went swimmingly—until we were ready to check out and I saw her. She was waving at me and I disappointedly realized, *Shit. I know her.* I had shopped here throughout my pregnancy and had chatted with several of the employees, lately informing them of the final countdown to baby. The last time I had seen this particular cashier, she had said, "Next time I see you, you'll have that baby in your arms." I knew she'd want to see Nella—to congratulate me—and I suddenly didn't know what to say. Do I tell her? Will she notice? Do I not say a word and have her notice on later trips to the store and wonder why I never said anything? I started to get uneasy, hugging the sling a little closer as she ran over to me to take a peek.

"Let me see, let me see!" She was in a full-out sprint to get to us.

I smiled as I pulled the sling fabric back and revealed this piece of heaven we'd been waiting for.

"Her name is Nella—" I stopped and watched as she took her in. And then, for some strange reason, I went on in this painfully seamless fashion, "—we found out when she was born that she has Down syndrome."

Oh, for God's sake, why did I have to say it? The cashier just stared at me—"Oh"—and then she didn't know what to say. It was obviously just as painfully awkward for her, and I suddenly felt really stupid, like I just muttered "I love you" to the boy I liked and he didn't say it back. I wanted to retract it, to tell him I didn't love him and that I certainly had never thought of what my name sounded like with his last name. I protectively pulled the sling back over my sleeping baby's face and looked down to find my embarrassment compounded by the two perfect round wet spots leaking onto my white shirt. I wanted to abandon my groceries and run like hell. Instead, I grabbed my dad two aisles over with his cart and whispered, "Let's get out of here . . . now." I filled him in on the scenario on the way out, and my dad, sensing humor was the answer, laughed and said, "Kelle, why don't you just get her chromosome studies laminated on cards and pass them out to anyone who happens to glance our way?" Point taken.

Now here we were—a week later—wiser, stronger, more weathered and yet I was still impressed with Joann's ability to hold my girl, show my girl, love my girl for all to see without the slightest hesitancy when I, her mother, wasn't quite ready myself. I would learn from her.

We walked through Target and I threw anything that screamed "cozy girls' week" into my cart. Firewood. Hot cocoa. Popcorn. If they sold log cabins, I'm pretty sure I would have bought one. I was just outside the ice cream aisle, ready to grab a half gallon of Rocky Road when I recognized a familiar face. She was young and pretty, and I realized I had met her only a couple weeks earlier when she had been called in to the hospital to come talk to a very sad mama who just had a baby with Down syndrome . . . me. Her name was Jennifer and, four years earlier, she had been that sad mama. I didn't really want to see her when she walked into my hospital room that day and, strangely, she probably knew that. So she sat quietly in a chair next to my bed and smiled. She told me everything would be okay and that if I had any questions I could call her. She gave me her card—the one I tucked into a place where I pretended I'd lose it but secretly, deep down inside, knew exactly where it was—and told me that support was available when I was ready. And I'll never forget what she told me before she left. "I don't know if this helps," she said, "but I have to tell you a little story. I have two boys. Jackson, who has DS, is the younger, but I have to tell you something about his older brother. We were at a base-ball game when the hospital called me today, and I told him I had to leave. When he asked why, I told him there was a mom who had a baby with DS who was sad and needed someone to talk to. He's used to this. I get called from time to time to do this. But today, he looked over at his little brother and said, 'I don't understand, Mom. Why are people sad about Down syn-drome?'" And then she leaned over and hugged me and congratulated me. As numb and emotionless as I was at the time, her story stuck with me and apparently, her pretty face did too as I now looked over and realized it was Jennifer pushing her cart next to me in Target, her older son walking next to her and her youngest, Jackson, sitting in the cart, smiling.

"Jennifer," I whispered. "Hi, I don't know if you remember me, but you came and saw me in the hospital a couple weeks ago." Her face soft-ened and a warm smile settled in.

"Of course I remember you. How are you doing?"

"I'm doing great." I gestured toward Nella in Joann's arms and saw admiration in Jennifer's eyes.

"This is my Jackson I was telling you about," she added, sweeping Jackson's bangs out of his face and patting his chubby hands, which were curled around the cart handle. "Jackson, this is my friend Kelle. Can you say 'Hi'?" Jackson laughed and shook his head, his fine hair whipping back and forth over his almond eyes and his soulful grin. I looked over at his older brother and made it a point to say hi.

"Your mom told me a lot about you too. So nice to meet you." I smiled and looked down at Lainey in my own cart, wondering what her world would be like four years from now. Jennifer and I said our good-byes and reiterated how fateful it was that we met again, and Joann and I continued our shopping, which, she later enlightened me, was really an unhealthy get-what-you-want spree for my eldest child. I'm sure it was the manifestation of my own disappointment and growing guilt for Lainey, who would unknowingly have to bear this new world of helping a younger sister with special needs. Apparently, I gave her everything she wanted that day, filling the cart with Popsicles, doughnuts, Pop-Tarts, Gummi Bears, a doll, two boxes of Dora Band-Aids, Lucky Charms, and a multipack of Bonne Bell Lip Smackers to boot. "I was worried about you," Joann later admitted. What, you don't give your child razor blades when they ask for them? I *could not* say no, and it became a deeper problem that affected me until a couple days after Joann arrived when I realized I had to do something about it.

It was late. We were watching a movie. Nella was jammied and fed, her tiny body nestled in Joann's arms. Lainey was likewise jammied and fed, her willowy body stretched across my chest, her blond head resting against my shoulder while she fell asleep. A fire crackled intimately and, as the room warmed and glowed, I felt the accumulated pain I had been storing begin to spill over.

"Joann?" I pleaded. She looked over and saw me crying. "Joann, I can't look at her."

"Look at who?" she questioned.

"I can't look at Lainey," I whispered as I gripped her a little tighter, feeling her sleeping breath against my neck. "I can't stand how bad it hurts. I can't even look at her without feeling so horrible for what she didn't get. I told her she'd have a sister who—" I stopped, dropping my head and letting this dark brew of guilt and pain overtake me for a minute. "She's not going to be able to do so many things I thought she would."

"Kelle, you are giving her so much more. She will be able to do so much with Nella—more than you think. You have to let go. She's happy. She's not sad, Kelle."

I shook my head and tried to let it out. Tried to face the demons I had locked up and thought about them one by one as I cried and held my firstborn girl against me—the one I had promised all these big sister dreams. I imagined Lainey, all innocent and pigtailed in elementary school—getting made fun of for her sister. I imagined her holding Nella's hand as they walked through a school hallway, waiting patiently for her little sister as her own friends ran by her. I thought of high school, dating, shopping, weddings, having kids. I thought of all the times I call my sister for advice, to laugh, to vent. I imagined what Lainey's phone calls would sound like and couldn't stand how much it hurt to think about it. The pain was sickening at that moment, and I needed an out.

"We're watching *The Hangover* again," I told Joann. I needed irreverent. I needed funny. I needed to laugh at something far removed from Down syndrome, and four guys getting wasted in Las Vegas seemed just the ticket. I slipped Lainey under the covers of my bed, kissing her cheeks repeatedly, hesitant to walk away but finally returning to the living room where I curled up next to Joann. I spread an afghan over both of us and settled into rehabilitating laughter within the first ten minutes of the movie. For a moment, things felt good. Halfway through the irreverent humor of drunk and stupid, I snuck away to get Lainey's baby book and returned to the couch where I wrote, without even explaining to Joann, as the movie continued. I wrote a letter to my daughter.

> Lainey, on January 22, you became a big sister and there are no words to describe what went on in my heart for you. It is a day that changed our lives and a day that will forever change yours. All the talks, all the books, all the getting ready we did with you—nothing could have prepared us for what we were told when Nella was born—that she was "different." One of my greatest pains that night was for you—everything I dreamed I would give you with a sister—it was all . . . different. What you'll never know is what you taught me that night. You showed me what love looked

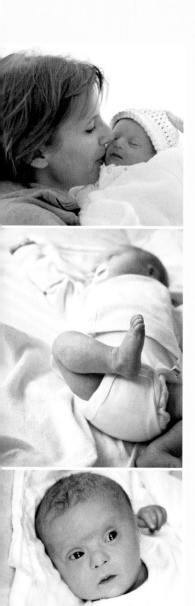

like. When I didn't know how to love, you showed me. You hugged her and kissed her and smiled so proudly and my heart ached that, at that moment, I couldn't give her what you did. Thank you for that, beautiful girl. We'll figure this out together. I love you more than you'll ever know.

I wiped my tears, placed the pen next to her book on the coffee table, and turned to explain to Joann. "Sorry, I really was watching the movie. I just needed to—" I noticed Joann's eyes were pooled with tears too.

"I know," she interrupted. "I was reading while you wrote it."

The letter I wrote to my daughter that night was healing and good, a closing chapter that, sure, might reopen from time to time but that put to rest feelings I needed to get over. I faced my pain and carried on. And the next morning, I happily welcomed the sunshine and my two beautiful daughters who needed me. Joann and I spent the next several days talking about just how amazing life is, with its intricate web of challenges and triumphs, and how we learn from all of it. We baked cookies in the afternoon with the western sun spilling into the kitchen and took long evening walks to the lake with the big tree that casts leafy shadows over the strong and hearty Florida grass.

Sadly, Joann would leave, but Brett was coming home. I was ready. I was ready for our family to be complete.

blueprint

WELCOME HOME, DADDY. I TRACED IT IN BIG LETTERS
on blue poster board and handed Lainey a fistful of markers to
color it in. She did, shy-smiling as she colored and finished up
with her own proclamation of a job well done. "Him gonna lub it,"
she whispered. "Him gonna be so excited to see us."

I had done it. I had managed to live through seventeen days
without my husband just a couple of weeks after I gave birth to
our second child. I had managed to muddle through heavy grief
holding a telephone with his voice rather than his hand and had
victoriously completed a half-month boot camp of middle-of-
the-night feedings, grocery store trips, toddler soothings, co-
ordinating my stepsons' homework schedules, and keeping a
house together without my husband there to help.

I loaded the girls and our decorated poster into my Jeep and
welcomed the relief that settled in a little more with every one
of those twenty-two miles to the airport—the relief that Brett
was coming home to complete our family. We arrived early, with
plenty of time to get a good spot at the entrance of the termi-

nal where incoming travelers greeted and hugged their loved ones. It was late, the airport was fairly quiet, and yet a small cluster of people had gathered to wait, many of them noticing my pigtailed girl eagerly dragging her WELCOME HOME, DADDY poster and my newborn snuggled in her sling. I suppose our little reception resembled that of a soldier's family, and I couldn't help but notice deep sympathy in others' eyes. *This poor young mom and these two fatherless girls,* they must have thought. I figured I wasn't going to argue that we had been through battle, and so I accepted their sympathy and waited for their confusion when they saw Brett walking toward us in a suit and tie as opposed to camouflage.

Oh, but it was still every bit a soldier's welcome. Tears pooled the moment I saw him, not just because I needed him but because I knew his eyes were locked on Lainey, and I felt her little frame unleash from the security of my legs and bolt toward her daddy, dragging the poster behind her. I felt guilty again for just a moment—thinking she must have needed something from him I couldn't give her—but then my joy and relief quickly swallowed the grief. I hugged him tight, burying my head in the crook of his neck, inhaling the familiar earthy scent of his cologne and suddenly feeling like everything would be okay.

"Would you like me to take your picture?" An older gentleman with white hair and a warm smile held out his hand for my camera, and I thanked him with my eyes as I wordlessly passed it to him. Yes, it was a moment, and he too sensed it needed to be captured. We clustered together as close as we could get, Lainey slung to the hip of her daddy on one side and a tiny Nella burrowed snugly into the crook of my arm on the other. We smiled as he counted—one, two, three—and *click*. It was the very first picture taken of all four of us together.

I realized soon after Brett returned there's more to feeling complete than just having every member of the family present. Sure, it felt a little more like home again in that I felt his body heat in bed at night and didn't have to explain to Lainey where her daddy was, but I still didn't feel completely settled, even with our family united. With Brett home I finally let go a bit, relinquishing some of my parenting responsibilities and allowing myself time to think. Before you build a house, construct a skyscraper, or erect the scaffolding of any major work of architecture, you plan it out on a blueprint. You sketch a drawing, assess it, then crumple it up and repeat the process—sketch, assess, crumple, sketch, assess, crumple—until you've finally perfected the prototype of something good, something workable, something of both form and function.

I spent the next several weeks drafting blueprints, sorting through the daunting heap of ideas, fears, and dreams that had accumulated in

my mind, trying to figure out how the hell I was going to do this. *What is our life going to look like?* I asked myself a million times. I wanted a model, a tangible thing I could see, a family prototype encased in glass just like the architectural models where Styrofoam cars are lined up in miniature parking spaces and painted trees fill landscaped lots. I wanted to see twenty years into the future and, at the same time, I was terrified to look. So I thought about it just about every moment I had alone. I cried while I lathered my hair in the shower. I got lost in thought while driving alone. I lay in bed in the dark at night consumed with what was happening.

It wasn't all about Nella, either. It was about me. There's another important part of growth that isn't as pretty as the first sprouts or the glorified moment a flower finally blooms. There's the pruning—the necessary cutting back of lush greens to reveal the raw and ugly insides of a stem. And yes, it seems antithetical to wait for a bloom and then chop it off once it has come, but it is purposeful, because what follows is even better.

I've never had so many philosophical discussions with myself in my life. I knifed away at so many feelings, so many perceptions until I felt completely broken. I asked myself difficult questions. *Do you care too much what people think? Are you hung up on perfection? How painful will this be? Why did this happen? Is this a coincidence or did God do this on purpose? For that matter, does God even exist? What kind of a God would let this happen?*

The last one grabbed me hard. Maybe having something life changing happen to you has nothing to do with God. Maybe it has everything to do with him. Either way, I took my brokenness as an opportunity to once again ask myself what I believed and why I believed it. I've been guilty of offering the same sympathy I'd been getting these past weeks when life throws a curveball. You know, the "Everything happens for a reason" and "Oh, God knew what he was doing" and, my personal favorite, "God chose you." While at first I nodded my head in agreement, I was beginning to wonder what that meant—that I was chosen. *What do you mean God chose me? Why? Because I deserve this? Because I'm such a freaking good mom that heartache would be the perfect reward?*

My dad calls them "God spinners"—those people who come in to every situation and spin it for God. You know, you go to buy a house and it falls through, and there they are, stroking your back and offering a pitying, "Oh, don't you worry, God has a better house for you." Yeah, but it doesn't always work. What if your husband dies? Are they there to tell you, "Oh, don't you cry, honey, God has a better man for you"? Because that's a surefire way for a grief-stricken wife to slap the hell out of someone and get away with it. Who really knows when and what God gets involved in? And that's not to say I don't believe that Nella was divinely destined to bless our lives. Sometimes it seems, looking back, that from the second I was born, events and moments were just carefully aligning in my life to prepare me for the second her eyes locked with mine in that birth room. And then sometimes it seems silly to think it's anything other than coincidence. Because good God-fearing folks lose their kids sometimes and sometimes wife beaters win the lottery. Who can explain that?

After a few good weeks of soul-searching, I decided it doesn't matter. I believe in God, but I also believe in science and coincidence and cause and effect, and somehow science and coincidence brewed together in the universe to twist some DNA, slap an extra chromosome on number 21, and rock my world on January 22, 2010. I could question it, fight it, and surrender to the flag of *It's not fair,* or I could learn from it. And I wanted to learn from it. I realized I was the only one who had the power to move on and turn our curveball into a home run, so I did my best to choose my perspective, shopping through all the imaginary aisles of packaged outlooks until I found the one I wanted. I wanted to change. I wanted to be better. I wanted to begin a journey of gratitude and growth, and this was the perfect opportunity. And so I pictured myself, on a hill, fist raised to thundering skies shouting to it all—to God, to the Universe, to Coincidence, to Science—"I see your challenge. I accept. I accept. I'll show you how I can do it. You have no idea just how I'm gonna rock this out."

Passion can overcome a lot and so can raising an imaginary fist, but we were still only a little into Month Two and there was more work ahead. More doctor appointments, therapy schedules, education, learning the ins and outs of Nella's care, and of course the normal two-kid mama things like balancing attention and letting go of guilt, or talking Austyn and Brandyn through all this. Then came the biggest challenge at the time—Brett's job.

Although he was working selling software remotely out of his own Naples office, he had been traveling a lot between Canada and the main office in Rockford, Illinois, the last trip taking him away for three long weeks. I'd always said I was the independent wife—the one who had plenty of things to do to keep her busy and fulfill her while the husband was gone and certainly not the needy one who cried herself to sleep at night missing him. Saying it and living it are two different things though. Hardship has a way of sending flares—drawing attention to the need for the family unit. Money had been tighter the last couple years and we needed Brett's job, but after Nella was born, I felt a throbbing need for togetherness. I wanted movie nights and board game Sundays, afternoon bike rides, and dinner around the table. Brett's being gone so much was just a big gaping hole in the protective ozone layer of our family.

If that wasn't bad enough, Brett hit me with the big bomb one night before he was preparing to head back up to Rockford.

"Babe, they want us to move to Rockford." He hung his head like the kid who just announced to his dad that he hit a baseball through the neighbor's window.

"You're kidding, right?" I laughed as I switched Nella from one shoulder to the next and patted her asleep. I knew it had been an option in the past. We had discussed the possibility of moving for his job while I was pregnant and had decided it wasn't possible with the boys unable to move with us. But now? The thought of uprooting our life and moving away from all these people we had just fallen more in love with the past weeks—the village that supported us and carried us through—made my stomach turn. After everything we had been through, the "wasn't possible" decision quickly changed into a big fat *absolutely no freaking way.*

"I wish I was kidding, but it's nonnegotiable now. If I'm going to keep this job, we'd have to move or I'd have to move by myself and travel back and forth or—" He trailed off and I sensed his stress and sadness as his voice wavered. I started to cry, and the presence of tears brought it all back again. The few mountains I felt I had already summited were now back again, and I suddenly felt small and incapable.

"No, no, no, we're not moving. You're not moving. We'll get rid of the house. We'll get a condo and all sleep in one bedroom. We'll sell everything, our cars, our furniture. No. Brett, I don't care anymore. I just want us. I want us to be together. Please, we can't do this. It can't happen, right?" I held Nella closer and used her body as a security blanket as my tears rolled onto the top of her head.

"We're not going to move." Brett said the words with a confidence I hadn't seen in a while. "I feel the same way. I just wanted to make sure you agreed."

And this is the place where the God spinners, if they were present, would swarm in promising that this was God's plan and this was all happening because certainly, there was a better job around the corner.

While Brett didn't land the job of his dreams, things did work out. He was given a little leeway time with his job while he looked for something else. Eventually, he scored some great side jobs managing properties while I picked up some professional writing jobs and did more photography gigs. We spent a lot of our savings in the meantime and pared down our expenses, settling on just one car between us, getting rid of my gas-guzzling Jeep as well as premium cable channels, extravagant cell-phone plans, and long Target trips where things outside of the grocery bill strangely made it into my cart. But we had *us,* and that meant everything.

I needed *us.* It was healing to be together, to be home, to hear laughter and watch movies and feel our everyday routine. I wanted the boys around more too. It's funny how things had changed. When I first married Brett, it was a challenge to change my expectations of my family dream and accept that the boys were part of my instant family. While I loved them as Brett's kids and strived to accept them as my own, there were times when I wanted alone time with Brett or felt disappointed when a planned romantic dinner turned into a boys-fest movie night where stinky soccer socks were propped up on our coffee table and the TV roared with fart humor and fight scenes.

Having my own kids changed everything though. Lainey loved her "bruh-bruhs," and they loved her, and my dreams of a big family were instantly satisfied with these amazing scenes of Austyn and Brandyn building forts for her with couch cushions or Lainey running to wake them up for school on Monday morning.

When Nella arrived, initiating my own falling-in-love journey with her was quickly followed by rallying to create at least a small close circle where she felt loved and accepted, like building a dam that would withstand everything else she'd have to face in life. It began with family, and while Lainey was easy—she loved her from the start—I wasn't sure how Austyn and Brandyn would handle the news. They were at the prime age where stereotypes and image were important, and I feared that suddenly having a sister with Down syndrome wouldn't be an easy pill to swallow. I wasn't present when they were told the news and definitely wasn't coherent enough even if I had been, but I am told there were two beautiful responses when they arrived at the hospital.

Fifteen-year-old Austyn wanted to hold her immediately and he did so with a gentle smile. Who knows what he was thinking, but while he held her, there was nothing but peace. While Austyn tends to be reserved and cool, holding his emotions on the inside and his magnetic biting wit on the outside, Brett was surprised later that night when he checked his phone to find a trail of text messages Austyn had sent to his friends.

"My sister was born. She has Down syndrome."

And the surprising response from these video-gaming, fart-humor-loving teens: *"You're kidding?! I'm sorry. How's Kelle?"*

"Not sure," he answered. *"Her name is Nella. She's so cute."*

For all the times I ever wished to have a night alone with Brett in the past, this exchange made me hope that Nella never has a night away from her brothers.

Brandyn's reaction was a little different from Austyn's. Eleven years old and far more emotional, he had a hard time coming to the hospital that first night. He hung on to his dad on the hospital bed, taking in Nella from afar and unable to control his tears. He cried the entire time, and everyone assumed it was because he was disappointed until Dot, our perceptive nurse and dear friend, took him for a walk down the corridor next to the nurse's station.

"What's the matter, buddy?" she asked when they were alone.

He buried his head in his hands and shook.

"I'm not crying because I don't love her," he answered. "I'm crying because I *do* love her, and I don't ever want anyone to make fun of her."

And because there were no God spinners present, let me take the liberty to spin this one. This here was God saying, "You better thank your lucky stars for these boys and this bond and for falling in love with a man with a built-in family. The best damn built-in family you could ever ask for."

As for getting made fun of, Heidi had that one taken care of. When she found out that was what Brandyn was crying about, she laughed. "Oh, for God's sake, that's an easy answer. Did you tell him I'll take care of that? You tell him if anyone makes fun of her, I'll personally put my foot up their ass!"

Best friends are great that way. If they're not leaving their kids to come lie in bed with you while your husband is gone and you cry yourself to sleep, they're promising to put their foot up someone's ass for you. That's true friendship.

SOMETIMES I WONDER WHAT IT WOULD HAVE BEEN LIKE to go through those first few weeks alone—without a supportive husband, siblings who loved her, a best friend who promised to kick some ass, a sister who picked up the phone in the middle of the night with a "What's wrong?," or a village of girlfriends who came with casseroles and open arms to hold her, to love us. And, in the intimidating new world of medical fears and questions, there was the comforting reassurance of having a pediatrician who not only gets life but who also gets an overly emotional mother.

Nella's first well baby appointment was easy. We talked weight and bilirubin counts, and I was out the door after a tearless half hour with a head circumference chart in my pocket. The morning of her second appointment, though, I was in knots. I knew it was coming—the pamphlets, the books, the "Okay, Kelle, this is what we'll need to worry about." Brett was working and I didn't think to take anyone with me, so I hauled both girls in the car, breaking in my "sea legs" as a mama of two on my own and feeling pretty brave because of it. Lainey fell asleep in the car, I forgot the stroller, and I couldn't bear waking up her tired little soul for her little sister's appointment so, once I arrived, I carried both kids—Lainey's sleeping body schlepped over one shoulder and a diaper bag and a car seat with a seven-pound, four-ounce baby in the other. I walked through the parking lot, breathing heavy and chanting to the rhythm of my jeweled sandals hitting the pavement, "I'm a rockstar. I'm a rockstar. I'm a rockstar."

Dr. Foley is, first and foremost, a mom. Dot, my OB nurse at the time (and later beloved friend), recommended her to me when I was pregnant with Lainey, and I knew the moment I met her that she was perfect for us. She has strawberry blond hair that tucks behind her ears and curls under with just the right approachableness to balance her role as both a smart, young physician and mother to four children. Her warm green eyes are trained to bring sympathy to scared, questioning mamas, and faint freckles paint her milky skin, bringing a comforting youthfulness to her confidence and experience. She and I were pregnant together for a moment, her with her fourth, me with my longed-for second before I miscarried. But then Nella came along, and there she was, our Dr. Foley, holding up the fort.

She was waiting for me that day when I walked in frazzled, hoisting a car seat, balancing a half-sleeping toddler over my shoulder, and holding the butterflies in my stomach at bay. And she, with her wisdom and experience and calming sage green eyes, smiled like she knew exactly what I was thinking.

"I'm nervous," I admitted. "Go ahead, hit me. Is this when all the info comes? What I have to look forward to? All the appointments and concerns and increased likelihoods?"

Dr. Foley tipped her head back and laughed. "Relax, Kelle! Everything's fine. Look at her, she's perfect!"

No one says "perfect" like Dr. Foley. I'd heard it so many times before from her—as a first-time mama, holding a jaundiced newborn, certain something was horribly wrong, and as a second-time mama, grasping to accept a painful diagnosis. Both times, she was there, smiling with her freckles and her green eyes and her strawberry blond hair, pronouncing "perfect" so effortlessly and genuinely with a little bit of a drawl on that first syllable to soften even more what was already, well—perfect.

"So here's the deal," she continued, smiling. "I'm supposed to give you some pamphlets on Down syndrome, but I know you and you're probably not wanting to read through a bunch of boring, blunt infor-

mation right now, so I read through them for you and took everything you need to know right now and wrote it down for you." She retrieved a small square of paper from her pocket, the size of a prescription tablet, scribbled with a few lines of black felt pen, and handed it to me.

"This is your to-do list for the next three years."

I looked at the paper, surprised to see only four instructions, each separated by numbers circled in pen.

1. Thyroid Screening, 6 months and once a year after

2. CBC (Complete Blood Count), 6 months and once a year after

3. Eye Exam by 6 months and once a year after

4. Spine/Neck X-ray by 3 years

I read each one carefully and stopped at number 2. I had read about Down syndrome being linked to an increased likelihood for childhood cancer a few weeks earlier, and I was paralyzed by the thought. "CBC, that's for leukemia, right?" I asked, nervously.

"Yes, but nothing you need to worry about. We already did her first CBC when she was born." Dr. Foley consoled. "Kelle, she's perfect."

"And this is it?" I pleaded. "That's all?"

"And lots of hugs and kisses," she finished.

I knew there was more in the future. But for right now, I had four things to worry about—that and some hugs and kisses, and I was more than capable of providing those. So I packed up my girls and drove home, where I taped the small square of paper with four circled to-dos to the side of the refrigerator and eventually forgot about it. I had memorized them anyway, could chant them in my sleep—thyroid, CBC, eyes, X-ray—but secretly hoped I'd forget and be so caught up in the beauty of life that someday, months down the road, I'd notice the crumpled piece of paper on the fridge, hidden behind Little Caesars coupons, and suddenly remember that, silly me, we have blood draws and eye exams to schedule. No big deal.

SOMETIME RIGHT BEFORE NELLA'S SECOND-MONTH birthday, the hospital bracelet I had worn since the morning I was admitted fell off. It was the last tangible thing I had that still connected me to that day, and I never could muster the courage to cut it off, which would have been like severing a bridge that allowed me to visit that place of "before" if I needed to go there. The plastic edges were frayed and the black writing that had once clearly spelled out my name had been worn nearly invisible, but still, every time I went to cut it off, it seemed I wasn't ready, as if some sort of grief course checklist had to be fulfilled first or maybe I just couldn't let go. And while I was waiting for that definitive moment when I felt this surging confidence to cut it off, I never felt it.

Confidence doesn't always come in surges. Sometimes—lots of times—it brews unbeknownst to us, building during the times we feel the least confident—through the tears, the questioning, the self-doubt, the begging God to make it better. Confidence, like contentment, is earned, paved stone by stone until you finally turn back and realize it has.all been pieced together to create something strong. Confidence is a process.

While I didn't feel a sudden influx of confidence, I smiled and recognized its presence one afternoon when I looked down to see the plastic hospital bracelet that had been hanging by a thread on my wrist finally fall to the kitchen floor. It was free, unleashed from the symbolic expectations it once held. I had anticipated tears with that final snip and yet here I was, holding a hungry baby and a can of tomato sauce, preparing to make dinner, and it happened right there in the middle of real life.

You gonna cry? I asked myself. I thought for a moment, tried to tap into some hovering grief just begging for the chance to spill, but I found nothing.

Nope. I'm fine. I smiled, picked up the broken bracelet, tucked it away in Nella's keepsake box, and returned to the kitchen, baby in tow, to finish my sauce. I felt confident—not naive enough to think the grief was over by any means, but content not only in that moment but in the fact that more grief would come. A severed hospital bracelet was not the last remains of an old life, but the celebration of merging into a new one with both more pain, but more joy as well. I felt lighter.

COINCIDENTALLY, MY BRACELET FELL OFF the day before march 21. March 21 is World Down Syndrome Awareness Day—an appropriate date, 3-21, for three copies of the 21st chromosome. I didn't realize this day existed, but as soon as I found out, just a couple weeks before it arrived, I knew I wanted to do something to celebrate Nella's life on that day. So we called the village together, to join us on the beach at sunset—the same beach where we celebrated Lainey two years earlier.

And celebrate we did, with a parade of people that lined up along the tide under languid skies. My obstetrician came. I hadn't seen her since Nella was born, and so we hugged and said the things you say at events like these. There were friends and family, neighbors and kids, and a heavy gray sky that hushed and froze as we gathered. It was surreal and sad and happy and celebratory and hopeful all at once. We said thank-yous and shed tears and made declarations to love and support her and change the world for her. I drank it all in, shielding Nella from the sea breeze and studying her features while my dad bellowed words and prayers and Brett squeezed his arm around my shoulder as Lainey rested her head on his. Nella wore the white baptismal gown my mom had made, the same one that was passed down from my sister's girls to mine, and she looked so small swallowed by all that lace and cotton.

Surrounded by the calming ocean and heavy gray sky, I realized, standing there with family and friends just two months after Nella's birth, that it still hurt. I could not deny that I still felt the throbbing pain of losing what I had expected. My friend Katie read aloud an essay that night—a well-known piece for special-needs parents titled "Welcome to Holland," which compares the experience of having a child with special needs to boarding a plane for Italy and finding out when you land, you've arrived in Holland. It goes on to say that Holland is beautiful too—different, but beautiful. There's a line at the end that says even though Holland is good, the pain of missing out on Italy will never, ever, ever, ever go away. And yes, there's one never and three evers. That's pain times four. As Katie read those words that night—*never, ever, ever, ever*—and I felt the weight of my new girl in my arms, my heart gripped with sadness once again. Yes, the pain was still there. I held Brett's hand and buried my head against his chest as my friend Andrea sang "Somewhere Over the Rainbow," and we watched as friends wiped tears and smiled.

We stayed on the beach until gray skies turned to darker gray and finally, almost black. But the real hope came after we left, when we all gathered back at our place, trading ceremony for laughter and candles and beer and music and passing jammied babies back and forth. We lit sparklers, poured wine, clinked glasses, and toasted to life and friends and, after a few beers, stupid things like cute shoes and good sex. We launched glowing sky lanterns into the air and gathered around the pool, watching them soar into the black sky as the echoes of laughter and music continued. It felt like everything I would have wanted to see encased in glass for a family prototype, an architectural model of sorts, at least the *Two Months Along* version. And here we were, on 3-21. It was nothing about Down syndrome, and everything about Life.

I decided, right then and there, that *that* would be my blueprint for this journey with my beautiful Nella. While there will be hundreds of moments when we will focus on Down syndrome and plenty of tears and fears to match, I hope that when it is all said and done, our journey will have been about Life.

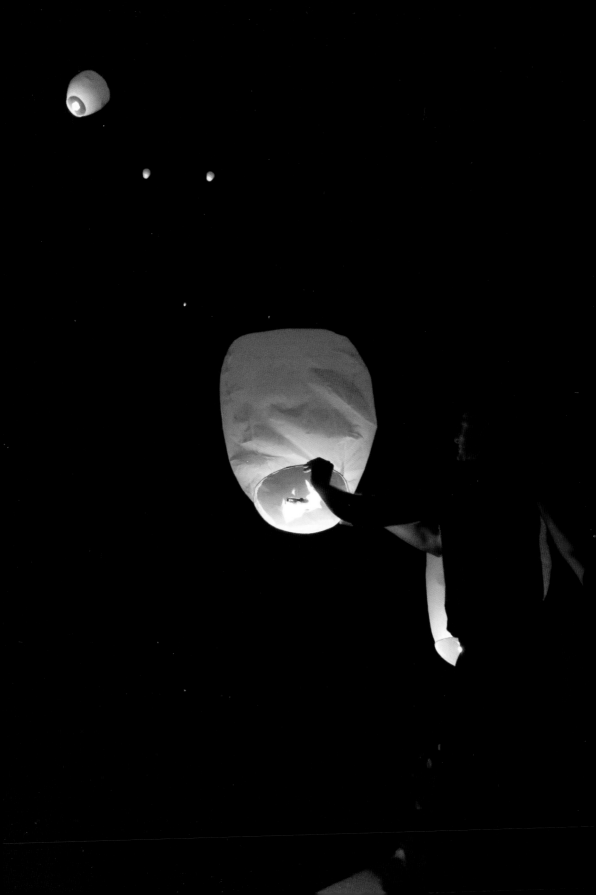

chapter 10

support

AMIDST MY GRANDER CELEBRATION OF LIFE, THERE were, of course, appropriate times to focus on Down syndrome. Try, say, when four therapists show up at your house at once to evaluate your baby. And one is pulling her arms and testing her reflexes, mumbling scores for each reaction while another who's set up a makeshift office at your living room chair is typing it all in. And you see the way your baby's head is a little floppy and how she doesn't turn to look at the bell that's being jingled outside her left ear and, although the therapist is quietly and professionally rattling off these number scores without alarm, you know damn well that "2" and "3" aren't the winning numbers.

So you hold it together—you really do—because even though you want to cry, you have an almost-three-year-old sitting on your lap wondering what the hell is going on, and you're explaining in some forced singsong voice, "See there? They're just playing with Baby Nella, just like we played with you" and "Oh, isn't that funny? Baby Nella's doing stretches." And while—at

this point, you have no idea that these therapists will later become your friends and will love your baby and that someday, you won't even frantically clean up your living room before they arrive—at this very moment, you want to cry and make a big scene, kicking paperwork and screaming, "For the love of God, leave my baby alone, take your portable office and your laptop and these goddamn bells and books and get the hell out of my happy house because I didn't sign up for this club and certainly, you've come to the wrong place."

It didn't go like that, really. Nella's therapists are good, caring people, and yes, they came and pulled her arms and rang their bells and rattled off numbers that were recorded into a laptop set up at a makeshift office. And yes, I held back tears and tried to explain to Lainey what it all meant. But I didn't kick or scream. I simply signed my name "here," "here," and "here," following the instructions of the therapists and scribbling where big X's on paperwork called for it. It was official. We were one of "those families"—thrown into our state's early intervention program and now the proud recipients of books on Down syndrome and packets full of information on disability acts and rights and camps and classes and support groups.

Support groups. I F-bombed just the suggestion of them in the hospital, as sitting in a circle with a bunch of moms I didn't know talking about my kid in terms of what she had rather than how I loved her wasn't my idea of helpful. I had my friends; I didn't need new ones, and I certainly didn't need new ones to "support" me—or so I thought. I recognize my attitude at the time was a defense mechanism, hovering near all I held to be good and true and pushing anything and everything foreign and intimidating away from me.

After I published Nella's birth story, I came around, though, the week of Mother's Day to be exact. I had been doing so well, shifting into a new acceptance stage. In fact, when a friend asked if I'd be interested in speaking at a local support group, I didn't even hesitate to say yes. I'm not sure what changed except I think I got ahead of myself after a few months of emotional progress. Kind of like those runners who wheeze through a two-mile run and suddenly think they're ready to sign up for a marathon. I guess I hoped my vulnerability and comfort with talking about everything might somehow help someone else, not to mention continue to propel me in my own acceptance journey.

Heidi accompanied Nella and me that Saturday morning, and as she drove us toward the church where it was held, I read aloud my prepared speech, a piece about the House of Motherhood and all its unopened doors and what lay behind them. We both cried in the car as I read it.

"Are you nervous?" she asked as we pulled into the parking lot.

"I think I'm okay," I answered. "It's gonna be great, right?"

"Totally." Heidi smiled confidently and yet I knew if I was the biblical David strapping on my scanty armor to fight Goliath, she'd be telling me it was going to be perfectly all right when she knew damn well I was gonna get my ass kicked.

I pulled a sleeping Nella from her car seat and took a short moment to drink her in before we walked in the door. Here we were, entering a support group because of this little unexpected blessing and yet her perfection at that moment, secured in my arms, made the idea of a support group seem so silly. I needed her though. I needed to hold her close as I hesitantly walked in that door, and I needed my friend next to me telling me it was gonna be great.

Three steps in the door, and I knew I wanted out. It was too early; I was too emotional.

Rows of industrial chairs lined one end of the church fellowship hall while a stretch of long tables filled another. Pamphlets on various Down syndrome information littered one of the folding tables like free samples at a pharmaceutical convention. I glanced down to find a brochure on *Mouth Disorders and Oral Hygiene* lying there, complete with detailed photographs of crooked teeth and receding gums. Nice. I turned away and looked toward the rest of the room. A large TV blared a scene from *Madagascar* for the kids in one corner of the room, except no kids were watching. There were kids though—most of them with Down syndrome. Two boys, maybe ten years old, sitting on the carpet playing a game. Two girls at a table helping a pretty red-haired baby with almond eyes in a high chair. A little blond-haired boy, maybe four, running around the room being chased by his brother. They were all beautiful—happy—and while I thought it might be uncomfortable for me to be around older children with Down syndrome so soon after our diagnosis, I was comforted by their presence. But something didn't seem right, and I couldn't put my finger on it. I looked at Heidi, and she instinctively sensed everything I was feeling.

"I want to go home," I whispered. I clutched Nella close and fought off warm tears that were beginning to well up. "I don't want to be here. *She* doesn't want to be here." I looked down at Nella and felt a wave of responsibility for her. "She needs to be home. Heidi, I want to take her home. I want to go home and watch a movie with Brett and Lainey. I want my house."

Heidi grabbed my arm and led me to a quiet corner. "I know. Oh, Kelle, I knew the minute we walked in the door. I knew you weren't okay.

Let's go. Seriously, you don't have to be here. You don't have to do this. You have every right to do what *you* want to do right now. I'll take care of it for you. I'll tell them you had to go. Seriously, just walk out the door and I'll take care of it for you."

"Heidi, I can't leave. I'm supposed to speak today. I'd look like a real asshole if I bolted now. I'm being ridiculous, really. I can do this. This is good for me." I started pacing, self-talking myself into a place where I wouldn't cry, wouldn't break down, wouldn't embarrassingly run out the door. I looked up and saw a familiar face.

I had met Holly a few weeks earlier when my nurse had suggested I get together with her. Holly had welcomed her fourth child, Brooke, just days after Nella was born and, although her family had prior knowledge of Brooke's Down syndrome, it was still difficult for them to accept. But, by the time I had lunch with her a few weeks prior, she seemed so at peace with everything. We juggled kids over sandwiches at a local café where we traded "how we found out" stories and casually threw our fears out into the void while we nursed babies and picked at our salads. As a fourth-time mom, everything seemed to roll off Holly's back with graceful ease, and her laid-back personality impressed me. When I saw her now at the support group, I walked over, searching for cues that suggested she might be as apprehensive as I was, but Holly seemed fine even though she still had difficult days ahead, with Brooke scheduled for cardiac surgery the following month. Holly rattled off something funny—although I can't remember what—and tipped her head back with laughter. She has a way of effortlessly inserting self-deprecating humor into a moment that calls for it, and at this precise moment, her attempt was calming. I wondered if she sensed I needed it, and I envied her strength.

We waited around for more moms to show up. A few of them did, quietly slipping in the door, their hesitancy visible through forced smiles and polite nods. One of them was Astra. Shortly after I published Nella's birth story, Astra had e-mailed me that she had read the story and thanked me for my honesty. She too had just delivered a little girl—her first one—and was shocked to find out her little Mia had that extra chromosome as well. Astra lived in Fort Myers, twenty minutes away, and when I was informed of the support group meeting, I thought it would be a great opportunity for us to meet. We had e-mailed back and forth, admitting our apprehension to go but agreeing it might be good for us. When I saw a shy-looking mama walk into the room alone, I knew it was Astra and I knew we'd be friends.

"Hi, are you Astra?" I smiled and gushed the most welcoming hello I could muster. I admired her bravery for coming alone, even without the security of her little one, when I was here to speak and could barely stay even with the added comfort of both my baby and my best friend.

"Hello, you must be Kelle." Her voice sang with a thick European accent, and I immediately felt connected. We hugged for a brief moment— one of those hugs that meant more than just a greeting.

"I was so hoping you'd bring Mia," I said, looking down at her empty arms and feeling sad that she didn't have the comfort of her baby with her.

Astra fished through her purse and pulled out a loose photo, bent at the corners. She handed it to me, and I smiled at the sight of a plump-cheeked baby, postbath, wrapped in terry cloth. Mia had beautiful round eyes—larger than Nella's—and her little tongue poked out of rosebud lips.

A small crowd gathered to look—Holly and Heidi included. We *oohed* and *aahed* at Mia's picture as Astra smiled proudly.

"You must miss her terribly," I projected, because certainly, I'd be aching for Nella.

"I do," she answered as she carefully slid the cherished photo back into a pocket in her purse, "but her daddy's taking good care of her right now." She glanced at Nella, and I knew she was missing her girl. "Can I hold her?" she asked.

"Of course," I answered, passing over a sleeping Nella. Astra's shoulders relaxed as she welcomed Nella and cradled her into a comfortable corner of her arms and began quietly singing a lullaby in another language. "This is what we sing to Mia," she added without taking her eyes off Nella. "It's from Lithuania, where I'm from."

A voice echoed across the room from a microphone, calling the meeting to order. I wasn't hungry but wanted something distracting that would keep me busy throughout the meeting, so I filled a plate with a pastrami sandwich quarter, a bag of chips, and a brownie while Heidi kept a protective eye on Nella.

"Do you want me to get her back for you?" she asked. "I know you want her. I can see it in your eyes."

Heidi was right. I was already uncomfortable to be here, and as I prepared to sit down and listen to the unknown and build the courage I needed to deliver something emotional, I knew holding Nella would soften the blow. But I saw Astra in the corner, oblivious to everything else in the room, softly singing to Nella, probably facing her own fears and missing her girl, and I couldn't do it. I knew if I was here alone, I'd run to hold a baby too, and I had a feeling Astra needed her more than I did at that moment.

"She's okay. I don't want to take her away from Astra. Look at her." We both turned and stared at the two of them, lost in the back of the room, and Heidi agreed.

"Well, if at any point you feel like you need her, let me know and I'll go get her for you."

The meeting began. Someone thanked us all for being there. Someone rattled off a few facts and figures. I picked up a pen to write some things down but instead wrote "This sucks" on a napkin and passed it to Heidi. She drew a picture of a naked man with a big penis beneath my "This sucks" and passed it back to me, laughing.

"Don't worry," she whispered. "I'll make you laugh."

I felt immature—really, I did. I mean, it's good to be uncomfortable in life, to challenge yourself to sit through difficult discussions that push you to think more, to be more, and yet here I was like a high school student writing notes in class and needing my friend to draw penises on napkins to pull me through. I looked around at the other moms who seemed to be intently listening, taking notes, nodding their heads, and all I could do was tune it all out and stare to the back of the room where Astra was holding my girl, humming Lithuanian lullabies.

Oh God, I was supposed to speak to these moms. I was supposed to stand up and rally and be some sort of voice of reason, and I didn't measure up to any of them. More important, I was supposed to *do* this—to be Nella's mom, to show up at these meetings and learn things that would help her, to intently nod my head and frantically jot down notes onto handouts that I would take home and study. I was supposed to be involved and wear this heavy coat of advocacy and know what I'm talking about. Just last week I had talked to another mom with a baby with Down syndrome and she threw out all these terms that were foreign to me, like "sandal gap" and "single palmar crease," totally expecting me to know them. I shook my head, smiling, and nodded, bullshitting my way through it and all the while feeling guilty that I hadn't hit the books or done the research. I pretended like I knew about that crease in her hand or the gap in her toes when really, I couldn't bring myself to get past the first page in the "What Is Down Syndrome?" chapter of *A New Parents' Guide to Babies with Down Syndrome*. And, since I'm confessing, my friend Marsha gave me a $100 Borders gift certificate that first week home from the hospital with a card that said "buy all the research books you need," and you know what I spent it on? Magazines. *Martha Stewart* and *Real Simple* and a small pile of feel-good classics for Lainey like *Paddington Bear* and *Owl Moon*. Oh, and a coffee. I bought a $4 caramel frappe thing with whipped cream and lots of little chocolate sprinkles.

I shouldn't be here, I thought. I wasn't like these other moms. I didn't know what I was doing.

Don't cry, don't you cry, don't cry, I silently chanted.

" . . . and we're grateful to have a member of our community sharing today," someone announced. "I'd like to welcome Kelle Hampton."

I looked at Heidi as I fumbled for my papers and turned away so I wouldn't cry. *Madagascar* rolled on in the background and still, no kids watching. I focused on *Madagascar* as I walked to the podium and thought about the little naked man Heidi had sketched just moments earlier.

Don't cry, I continued to chant to myself.

I unfolded my papers and nervously smoothed them out against the wood of the podium. And I read. . .

> "About this time last year, I was given a key. It was a beautiful key—heavy and gold with intricate scrollwork and extravagant edges, a fine match for the collection of keys I had already acquired in my House of Motherhood. And for nine months I held that key, felt its weight in my palms, rubbed my fingers along the end that would open the door to a room in my heart whose glory I was about to discover. I dreamed of that room—how perfect it would look inside, how the light would filter through the windows, how each corner of its blessed walls would hold so much happiness someday. I imagined the things people would say when they walked into that room . . . things like, 'Oh, what a beautiful room' and 'How I wish I lived here.'
>
> "I waited patiently and passionately for the day I could use my key to unlock the door to the beauty which was to unfold in that room. And on January 22, I turned the heavy key into the lock of the door that separated me from that room and opened it to find something I didn't think I wanted to find."

I stopped and looked up. I saw Heidi's eyes glued to me, smiling, and the little red dot from the tiny video camera she held in her hands. I scanned the room quickly until I saw Astra in the back, rocking my little girl, and I choked. My throat burned and tightened, and when I tried to speak, my voice squeaked and cracked. I stared at the words on the paper as they quickly blurred and watched as hot tears dripped, dripped, dripped onto ink that began to run.

I wanted to go home. I wanted to hold Nella. I wanted to be sitting back at the table watching Heidi draw inappropriate things. But I went on. I thought I was okay, but I realized as I spoke to all these other moms on this journey with me, there was still so much pain. Maybe I'll

always cry at moments like these, even years down the road. Maybe the pain never goes away. Or maybe it does. Right then, though, I felt silly for being so emotional, overly moved by it all when everyone else seemed to have it figured out. I questioned myself, as I looked up from my speech again—heart throbbing, throat tightening, coughing out words through gasping attempts to hold back tears—to see these other moms more put together, fishing out chips from Frito-Lay bags and picking tomatoes off their sandwiches while they scanned through all the informative brochures while I spoke. Maybe they knew something I didn't. Maybe I had a long way to go.

I don't know the answer, but I do know I was relieved as I turned the page to read aloud the last paragraph.

> "I didn't know that just a few short months ago . . . the room which startled me with its unfamiliar colors and design would soon be a place of comfort, of beauty, a place with secret passages that lead to other rooms in the House and connect us in ways we didn't know existed. But, looking at my House now, with all its experiences, with its lived-in rooms, with each precious, cherished family member and the memories they will bring to these hallways, to these spaces, I wouldn't have it any other way.
>
> "And we can say it together today . . . Oh, what a beautiful House. How glad I am we live here."

I returned to the table and made a conscious effort not to sigh aloud. Heidi's face was red and tearstained, and she mouthed the words *that was beautiful* as she closed the video camera. An attractive Latina woman named Eliana who had two children with Down syndrome followed me at the podium and before she began, she thanked me aloud.

"I remember that emotion, I remember that pain," she said. And then she smiled and tapped her chest and locked eyes with mine. There was silence for just a moment, but I heard her through her smile—a wordless "It's going to be okay." She went on to tell a cute story about her little boy and how much like typical children he was. He, at four years old, had asked her for an LCD. Confused, she had asked him to explain, and he led her to his room where he pointed to his old TV and clarified, "This is trash. I want LCD."

I joined the others in laughter that felt good and healing and tried to calm myself for the remainder of the meeting.

Someone else shared information—things we needed to know, numbers to call, laws and rights and things we'd have to fight for. I started to get the idea that once our kids hit three and were released from the Early Intervention program, it would be hell getting what we were owed. "You're going to have to fight," they told us. I tried to imagine Nella three years down the road, dropping her off at a real school, in a classroom with other kids like her. I imagined meetings in school boardrooms where experts held fat, rubber-banded folders filled with papers and evaluations typed with "Nella Hampton" as if she was just one among many—student number 7, the one with Down syndrome. I didn't like it. I didn't believe it either.

And right there, posttears, I began to feel a passion, an enraging powerful passion that sank deep into my bones and flushed my cheeks. No, no, no, I wasn't going to go about it like this. I wasn't going to walk into this guns ablazing, expecting that everything was going to be so much harder for Nella. I had taught in this county for three years and was confident that the school system would do its best to serve my child, but it was my responsibility in the end. It felt good to own it. I would fight for Nella's rights just as much as I fight for Lainey's and that's whatever amount of fighting it takes to make sure that my kids get the best damn education they deserve. Hell, there's just as much of a chance I'll be sitting in a boardroom looking over papers typed with Lainey's name—one among many—as there is with Nella. And either way, it doesn't matter. They're *my* kids. It's *my* job to raise them. And sitting here years before we'll possibly even cross that bridge, worriedly anticipating how we're going to handle the school system leaving our kids hanging was not how I wanted to be spending my Saturday. I was her mom, and I was confident I'd figure it out.

I waited for the meeting to end as I practiced writing my name in cursive on the back of my handouts and traced over them with my pen until the paper wore thin where I had written. All the while I tried to make sense of it all, amending my blueprint for this journey where necessary.

The meeting finally adjourned, and I bolted to the back to get my hands on Nella. Another mom I had coincidentally met a month earlier at the park came over to me, eyes wide, face white.

"This wasn't easy," she said. "I don't know that I'll come again."

"Lisa, all I want to do is go home," I admitted. "It's not just you, if it makes you feel any better. That was really rough. Maybe I'm just not ready." She looked relieved. We made plans to call each other as she gathered her girls and left, and Heidi and I threw our stuff together, bundled Nella, and made a mad dash for the door. We had planned to meet Astra for a drink at a restaurant nearby, and as we drove, Astra following us, I let it all out in the car—the best friend therapy session, sans alcoholic beverages.

"I felt like I knew what I was doing, Heidi, and now?" I paused and threw my hands in the air for dramatic effect. "I feel like I just slipped back again. I don't know how to do this, and that just freaked me out," I blurted. "I just love her, that's all I know. I love her so much, I'd do *anything* for her—*anything*, Heidi—and if it's going to be as hard as they say it is, that's fine. Really, I'm on board for all of it, but can we not take one step at a time here? I have a baby. I have a brand-new baby, and I want to talk about how amazing she is. I want to feel like a new mom and gush over how long her eyelashes are and how she gets all breathy and excited before she eats. I deserve that, right?"

"You totally deserve that," Heidi adamantly agreed, but then again, she would have agreed with anything I said at that point.

I MAY NOT HAVE LOVED MY FIRST SUPPORT group meeting, but my second support group meeting was just what I needed. The second commenced just moments after the first one. Oh, we didn't have handouts or guest speakers. But we had three friends—me and Astra and Heidi—and a sleeping baby, and two Coors Lights for Heidi and me—extra limes—and a cosmopolitan for Astra—"my very first one since I was pregnant with Mia," she announced before she tipped it, sipped it, and set it down with a smile. "Delicious," she whispered.

Our support group continued over artichoke dip. We settled deeper into the leather cushions of our booth. We laughed louder. We told stories about how our babies dreamily looked at us when they first woke up, about how we lived for their breathy coos. We got quiet and shook our heads in agreement when one of us said there was something strangely enchanting—almost otherworldly—about locking gaze with our almond-eyed ones. We said we didn't care—that we were happy to be on this journey. We said we still hurt—oh yes, we hurt, but that we loved so much deeper than the hurt and that in itself was empowering.

"Mia is Mia," Astra finished confidently, "and we don't care about the rest."

"Yes," I quietly repeated, "Nella is Nella, and the rest, we'll deal with when it comes."

And then we said good-bye.

Had it been a real therapy session—one we paid for—a licensed therapist might have watched us and listened while he nodded and pursed his lips and scribbled diagnoses in our charts—words like *fear* and *denial* and *grief*. Maybe some of those were true. Someone left an anonymous comment on my blog soon after Mother's Day telling me I was in denial—that this cute little baby stage where everyone loves my kid would end soon and that it was going to get way worse and that maybe I'd come to grips with the fact that I'd been royally screwed in life when I threw my blue skies and rainbows away and admitted, years later, that this indeed was a hard, unfair life.

Well, that just pissed me off. And for a second, I wondered if it was true. I questioned my place on this journey and worried that my blueprint would result in a disaster, like the caveman's square wheel that went nowhere.

So I decided I would face it, the beast of information. Knowledge is power, right? I didn't want to read the books, to do the homework, but I knew it was time. I couldn't soften the blow with cute little napkin drawings or summoning the village to hold my hand while I read. I couldn't have a book party where we all drank beer and ate chips and salsa, taking turns reading intimidating lines from *A New Parents' Guide to Babies with Down Syndrome* and throwing down a shot afterward. This wasn't anyone's job but mine. After all, I was Nella's mother, her advocate, the one responsible for dealing with her future.

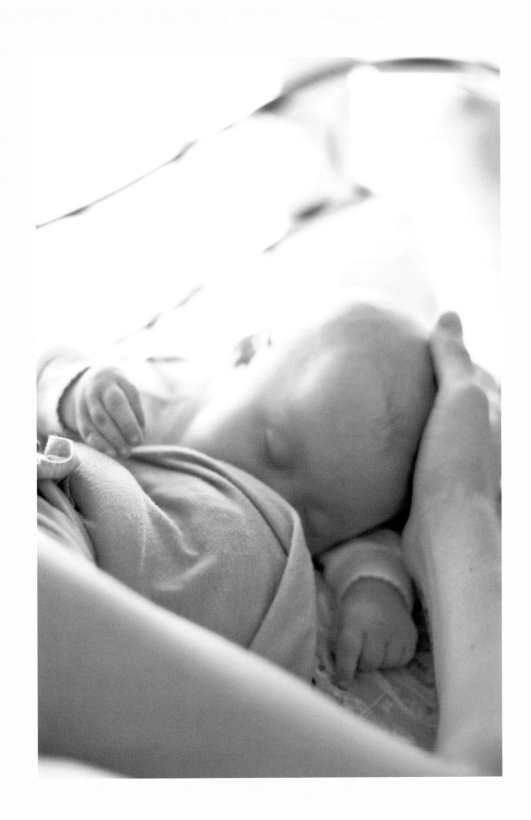

I did it alone one night. The house was black, well after midnight, and everyone was asleep. I sank into my desk chair, uncertain and afraid, and stared into the bright glow of my computer as I clicked on the first site, a safe one for starters, www.pubmed.gov, a service of the U.S. National Library of Medicine. I typed "Down syndrome" in the search bar. Twenty-four thousand articles pulled up, and I scrolled past the first ones full of daunting genetic terminology until I found something in a layperson's terms. It was factual and emotionless, easy to read compared to what I had expected. I trudged on, googling phrases and terms I had learned the past few months and clicking on links that led me to organizations and forums delving into fears other parents had. I learned what a sandal gap was, the large space individuals with Down syndrome have between their first two toes, and that babies with Down syndrome usually sport an extra line down the centers of their palms called a single palmar crease. In between surfing Down syndrome sites, I pulled my *New Parents' Guide to Babies with Down Syndrome* from the secret place where I had stashed it and flipped through the pages, holding it close to my screen so I could read.

I already knew about a lot of the things I was reading from some of the early information I sifted through in the hospital, but somehow studying it alone, completely submerged and devoted to the purpose of gaining insight and strength, made things seem more real. And it wasn't easy to read.

Chances for leukemia and Alzheimer's and seizures and surgeries and infections and heart problems are greater with Down syndrome, the sites say. And they say that life expectancy averages around fifty-five, too. Fifty-five. I repeated it out loud and quickly did the math in my head. I'd be eighty-six years old, likely still alive. Would I bury my child? Would Lainey be welcoming her first grandchild and saying good-bye to her sister at the same time?

I cried as I read on, clicking from site to site, my eyes glued to the screen. Hours passed, and I found myself soon engrossed in forums, reading about children who didn't make it, babies with almond eyes and steroid-induced moon faces undergoing their first round of chemo. I forced myself through stories of mothers who were fighting school systems, dealing with playgroup moms who didn't want their kids at parties, watching as all the neighborhood kids left the swings at the playground to find something better, and accepting the fact that their kid got left behind because she couldn't keep up. I could have turned the computer off at any time, but I couldn't stop, instead sinking further into these disturbing hours of torture like some sort of emotional cutting ritual. I knew a girl in college who used to cut herself. She said her life was so painful that cutting allowed her to wake up and escape the numbness. She said that after a while, it didn't hurt and that a strange sense of victory and control came from the point when she cut and didn't feel it.

I kept reading, waiting for when it wouldn't hurt, like sprinting through the point when your side is cramping and your legs are throbbing. But you keep running, wincing and gripping, doubled over until you reach that place where you're weightless and you pick up speed and the throbbing dissipates, leaving you a gazelle, propelling toward victory.

"Run harder," I said as I forced myself. I wanted to be a gazelle. And so I read on. "More painful, more frightening," I demanded, thinking certainly I'd be stronger because of it. I'd desensitize my fears until the cuts didn't hurt.

That's when I pushed myself too far. I read comments on YouTube clips from Special Olympics. I read what they said about the talent show where a girl with Down syndrome was singing and dancing and smiling. I read the horrible things people said and pictured my Nella.

They called the young girl a retard. They made jokes about her almond eyes and her soft nose and her beautiful stubby fingers. They said things that were too painful to repeat here, and I felt a hurt so deep, so raw—like the night I writhed in pain on the hospital bed trying to come to grips with our new life. I held my sides and shook silently as I forced myself to read the words again. *Retard.* I said it out loud, picturing my beautiful child, and I cried until I had no more tears.

Sometimes, when you run hard and fast and your sides scream with pain, it's because you need to stop. Sometimes, when people cut themselves, relief doesn't come with the next cut but rather they slice too far, severing critical blood flow that keeps them alive.

I cut too far that night.

Hearing painful things is never easy, but I have acquired a sense of understanding. After that torturous night of reading truly hurtful things that, in reality, exist in this world, I am at a place where yes, it stings a little, but it stings less for my child because I know who she is and what she is capable of. Words are merely words—meaningless unless given power to affect us. It does sting, however, to know that the world is full of pain—pain that people harbor inside and lash out, projecting their hurts onto the undeserving.

The Down syndrome books have a place in our home now, stacked neatly in an old suitcase on our coffee table where they are retrieved periodically for quick reference. I know they are there along with all the websites and forums and support groups, ready to inform and enlighten me if I ever decide that's what I need. But that night, all I needed was the presence of my family.

I finally escaped to bed, although it was nearly daylight. Moonlight poured through our back window, illuminating Lainey's little body snuggled close to Brett and providing a welcoming reprieve from my pain. Right before I slid into the sheets to join my family, I leaned over the bassinet butted against my side of the bed and stroked Nella's hair.

Let the pain fuel you, I told myself. *Feel that sting and move forward.*

I leaned farther, pressing my cheek against hers and reaching to take her chubby hands in mine.

"I love you," I whispered to her. "We'll figure this out, baby. We'll figure it out and take one step at a time."

She sighed and repositioned until she was comfortable and breathing deeply again. And I slipped my tired body into cold sheets, turned into my pillow, and fell asleep just as the sun was waking up.

chapter 11

the current

IT TOOK ME A LITTLE WHILE TO SHAKE THE FEELINGS
that arose in me the night I forced myself to "go there," but
eventually I did. Perhaps it wasn't so much that I shook them,
but I at least acknowledged their presence in my mind. My
cousin Heather says bad emotions need a little hug before you
let them go. Of course, I tend to take things to the moon, so I
not only hugged Fear and Sadness that night at the computer,
but I let them unpack their bags and stay awhile. I left them
little trial-size shampoos and let them wear my favorite pajamas. But, a few days into the embrace, I realized that they
had no intention of leaving. My mind was trailing back to the
things I had read a little too often, and I was weary from feeling
the guttural lurch of my insides every time I pictured someone calling my child a retard or envisioning hospital visits
and end-of-life care before it was a fair time to say good-bye. I
was having trouble controlling my emotions, and I realized it
was my own fault for laying out the red carpet so welcomingly

for the duo. Fear and Sadness had to go, and it would be my job to kick them out.

Sometimes, you have to have these conversations out loud with yourself, like my silly stress management ritual when I count to ten while I grip the steering wheel after sitting through the third red light in Florida tourist-season traffic. And so one morning, after a lousy start to my day, I did. I just said, "Get out," loudly and forcefully, like a true badass, if I do say so myself. "I am not afraid. So get the hell out of my head. *Now.*" I imagined them feebly recoiling, Fear huddled behind Sadness, before they skittered out. And the more I thought about it, the quicker they ran. In my head, I stopped Sadness at the door, pinning him against the wall, pointing my finger hard to his nose before he had a chance to beat it. "And I want my pajamas back, dammit," I demanded. Because I *am* a badass.

While I was very vocal and open about my emotional breakdowns and consequent recoveries, Brett was more reserved about his. Since the moment Nella arrived that January, other than finding my husband tearfully scouring the garage for a heater for her first bath, Brett only

had one breakdown I had witnessed. It was random and seemingly trivial, but most likely tremendously purposeful in that he had restrained a lot of emotion and pushed it down beneath the surface. In assuming a fatherly role of strength and support, his emotions had built up to the point that the slightest scratching of the surface threatened to unleash them. I'll never forget the moment it happened. I was sitting at my computer a couple of months after Nella was born, Lainey was asleep, and Nella was resting in a Moses basket near my desk. Brett sat down near me and began making small talk while I typed, and Brandyn eavesdropped from the kitchen. I was only half listening, not even looking at Brett while he talked, but I was jolted out of my computer-focused haze when, out of nowhere, he quietly asked, "Hey, Kelle, will Nella ever be able to walk to a friend's house by herself?"

I stopped typing and turned my body to face him, noting his failing attempts to suppress tears. My heart sank as I struggled to fight back my own tears, convincing myself that the two of us were never allowed to be sad at the same time. This was my turn to be strong for him.

Play cool. Don't let him know you're sad.

"What do you mean, babe? Like will she be able to walk on her own a couple blocks in the neighborhood?" I could think of a hundred worse things I could cry and worry about when it came to our future, but for some reason this one was hitting Brett hard. "Is that really important to you?" I asked.

"Yes. I really want her to be able to do that. I remember"—he struggled to finish—"when the boys could finally walk in the neighborhood on their own, I thought it was the coolest thing."

Brandyn walked out of the kitchen, saw his dad crying, and ran to sit on his lap. Brett wrapped his arms around him while I sat, struggling to think of something consoling, watching the two of them, bodies shaking, tears streaming, clutching each other for comfort.

I didn't know what to say. For the first time, I wished there was some sort of Down syndrome hotline on speed dial for these questions. I thought about googling "Down syndrome and independently walking

in a subdivision" but figured I wouldn't have any luck. So I did the best I could on my own. Choking back tears, I answered as calmly as possible, "I don't see why we can't hope for that. I mean, maybe she'll do it a little later than when the boys did it, but I don't know why we couldn't teach her to safely get somewhere and call to make sure she made it." I hadn't even thought of this myself. Was this the kind of thing that would later make me sad? And, for a split second, I felt it too—what Brett felt at that moment—but as quickly as it came, it left. "Babe," I went on, "so what if she can't? So we walk her a couple blocks if she wants to go play. Is it really that important? She's got older brothers and a sister who can help get her there and, in the grand scheme of things, this isn't a big deal, right?" I felt guilty for not validating his pain as much as maybe I should have. I mean, for God's sake, this was the first time he really lost it. But it worked.

"You're right," he answered. "It doesn't really matter, and I'm going to work really hard to teach her how to do it if she can." I walked over to the basket where Nella was sleeping, leaned over to scoop up her little flour sack body, and carried her over to where the boys were sitting to join them. And then we all circled around her and talked about all the things Nella *would* do. Like walk and talk, get in trouble, take ballet, get into Lainey's things, borrow clothes, snuggle on the couch, and watch favorite movies—the list went on.

"So, she'll recognize us, right?" Brett asked as we finished. I was stunned to think that all this time, maybe that was actually a fear of his.

"Babe! Of course she'll recognize us. She does now." I looked down to see my girl, snuggled a little more comfortably against familiar skin, and realized maybe Brett needed a crash course in Down syndrome. Suddenly I began digging up books in my drawers and rattling off information, some daunting, some hopeful. About two sentences into my lecture, though, he stopped me.

"No, I don't need any more. I don't want all this information. I just want to love her. I want her to show us who she is, and I'm perfectly okay with that."

"Are you sure?" I figured it was one of those times (many, in my book, of course) where I knew better than him. "Because there's a lot of stuff I could tell you that I think would make you feel better."

He smiled confidently. "From now on, if you think there's something that's important for me to know, that's fine. Tell me. But, I promise, I'm okay. I don't want to be bombarded with information. She'll show me what she can do. I'm not even really sure why this made me sad tonight. No matter what she's able to do, we'll be fine. We just love her, right?"

I so loved him at that moment and would have renewed my vows right there in our living room if I could have. We just love her. How easy was that?

Here's the cool thing. There's a yin and yang to everything, and when yin has you down, yang seems to deliver. For example, while Down syndrome brings with it unexpected challenges—like a life full of therapy visits—our case came with a few silver linings, like a physical therapist named Jonah who happens to be a little bit hot. Everyone knows the agonizing experience of a root canal is made easier if the dentist performing it looks like George Clooney. Well, therapy is a little bit the same.

Setting up therapy is an ordeal. After the initial assessment that includes a team of therapists evaluating your child, you wait for the call that tells you, yes, your kid meets the requirements for therapy (even though you already know she does), and someone will be in touch telling you what therapist you've been assigned to. Like you just walked in to Supercuts and are waiting for the first stylist to finish her blunt cut so you can take the next chair. Would you get the best? Or would you get a stylist who doesn't know what she's doing, so maybe you'll end up looking like Lloyd Christmas for a few months before it grows out? What happens if we got a bad therapist? I wanted to trust the system, I did, but, at the same time I wanted to slip a twenty into the palm of our coordinator, wink, and whisper, "You'll get her the best one, right?"

Thankfully, our "people" were nice. Really nice. They told us Nella had been assigned to a new therapist who had just moved here from L.A. And the morning of her first official physical therapy appointment, I ran around like mad, shoving clutter into drawers and hidden closets.

"Dude, throw out the beer bottle," Brett said, pointing to an empty Coors Light on the counter from the night before. "You know these people are really in here to check up on what kind of parents we are." Of course Brett would think this because he also thinks the random middle-of-the-night plane we hear flying over our house is on a secret government mission of mysterious importance. I raised my eyebrows and gave him the "Oh, really?" look.

"I'm just sayin'," he retorted, grabbing the bottle and chucking it into the recycle bin.

The small responsible part of me had made sure Nella was fed and rested for her first therapy visit, while the mama bear voice within me pleaded with her to do well. *Show him what you got, kid. You can do this.* As much as I was completely grateful for state programs that funded free therapy in our home, the *maybe-this-isn't-really-happening* part of me imagined our first visit would leave the PT completely confounded as to how amazing she's doing and he'd proclaim a glorious victory and give us a free pass out of therapy.

I was smoothing a blanket on our playroom floor when I heard the rumblings of a Harley pull into our driveway. Hmmm. Interesting. And here I thought all therapists drove Corollas.

I patted the few thin wisps of Nella's hair down with some butter-milk lotion in a last-minute attempt to make a good impression. We had already prepped Lainey in a moment of special-needs-parent-sibling-guilt with some bullshit story of how someone "kinda like Dr. Foley" would be coming over to do a "checkup" on Nella and that he really, really wanted to meet her awesome big sister, too. So, thankfully, the big sister was excitedly anticipating a random house visitor and an amusing interruption to an otherwise ordinary day.

Brett parted the blinds and attempted an inconspicuous peek-through. "Um, dude, come check this out. This guy doesn't look any-thing like a therapist."

Jonah was at the door by the time I came to spy, and I tried to hide my "oh wow, you're surprisingly kinda hot" face when I greeted him. I'm not sure what I was expecting, but I figured the person who stepped out of the imaginary Corolla wouldn't exactly have a strapping shirt-ripping set of biceps on him.

Jonah is a best-of-both-worlds cross between Arnold Schwarzeneg-ger and Matt Damon, but what's most pleasantly surprising is that be-hind the shell of his überbuff physique and chiseled jawline, he's a protective teddy bear. Within seconds, he was lying on the floor, shoes kicked off, head rested next to Nella's and one arm hooked around her tiny frame.

"Hey, little buddy," he nudged. "You're pretty cute." For the next hour I watched as Jonah gently coaxed her head from side to side and flexed her tiny legs into different positions, all the while nonchalantly keeping a steady stream of conversation going with me and Brett, like he knew we were anxious. And, perhaps sensing we needed more, he went on to share about how incredible all his patients with Down syndrome have been—how much they make him laugh, how they've bonded, how he taught them how to walk. "You know, sometimes kids don't like therapy and they get mad when they see me walk through the door because they know I'm going to make them work," he said as he gathered his things together to leave, "but Nella here? I have a feeling she and I are gonna be close buds."

And so it was. Week after week, Jonah arrived, making a fuss over Lainey before he made his way to the playroom floor where he'd kick off his shoes, drop to the carpet, and scoop up his little patient. It wasn't long at all before it felt completely normal in an almost *family-stopping-by* kind of way. While he rotated her hip joints, I'd pour him a cup of coffee—black—and he'd ask me how the pie I was making on his last visit turned out. And while coffee and pie-making discussions might step

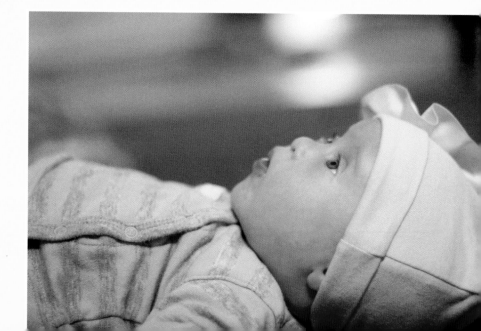

outside the structured professional responsibilities of a government-appointed physical therapist, I wouldn't have it any other way. Government funds grant us a folder in a system where we get therapy just for having a diagnosis, but I want more than a patient number stamped on a folder. I want personal connections. I want you to know our child—our family—and I want to know you. I want you to know what her favorite color is, what nickname she responds to, and that her tambourine is her favorite toy; and likewise, I want to know how you take your coffee, what your kids' names are, and what you got your wife for Christmas. I love my child something fierce, and if you're going to help us get her to walk and hold herself up, I want you to feel that too—what it's like to want her to succeed, to love her so much you'd do anything. You can't get this by crossing off the government checklist, but you can begin by serving a cup of coffee to the therapist who'll be walking in your door every week for the next three years and letting him know that you care a whole hell of a lot about personal relationships because that's where things get accomplished. I wanted Jonah to know we cared, and you know what? He cared too.

The ease with which we settled into a therapy schedule was just a small testament to the greater settling that eventually happened in our minds—gradually, of course, and without even realizing it. Someone let

go of our bike, and we were pedaling, smiling, holding the handlebars without the white-knuckled grip that had characterized the first several months of our new life. We didn't even realize we had been let go, but we were gliding, and about the time Nella was five months old, I had to remind myself that things weren't any different than I had expected them to be back when she was folded within my large round belly and I dreamed of what Lainey's little sister would be like. I had to remind myself that she had Down syndrome . . . because I was beginning to forget.

People ask me *when* it happened and *how* it happened—that I became okay with a special-needs child, that the "she has Down syndrome" alert that used to chirp its notification every day, on the hour, eventually faded, followed by the advent of contentment, even joy. People ask when and how the fear disappeared.

Evolving as a human being takes a lifetime. There is no definitive answer, no calendar celebration of the day a "new and improved me" arrived; no packaged instructions or a nice how-to-get-there guide. There is no moment the respirator tube was pulled out and loved ones watched anxiously as I choked and gasped and shifted suddenly into breathing on my own. Likewise, there is no promise that Fear and Sadness won't return, just as there is no promise that I'm free sailing through motherhood in general or even through my marriage. Grappling with any new challenge in life is like learning to swim. In the beginning, it damn near feels like you're drowning. But you exhaustedly flail and flap and kick to survive. Slowly, you learn to tread water, and though moving forward might mean clutching the wall of the pool like a toddler and scrambling your fingers along the edge, you move. Eventually, you tread water and graduate to new strokes, and finally, after flailing and flapping, after clambering and slowly scooting, after experimenting with backstrokes and breaststrokes, you find the current and let go.

I remember some sound advice I once heard about letting go. I was twelve, and we had joined my best friend, Tisha, and her family for a three-week voyage to the great American West. It was an adventurous trip, one that granted us rare opportunities—like soaring over the steep crevices of the Royal Gorge in a tiny tram car, climbing craggy trails up Pike's Peak, gripping the edge of our raft as it bounced around like popcorn against wild rapids along the Colorado River. I was scared of the latter adventure, I have to admit. White-water rafting was risky and dangerous. But, like most twelve-year-olds attempting to prove their own fearlessness, I suppressed my hesitation as I tightened the strap of my helmet.

Our tour guide was a young woman, obviously far past the stage of having to prove her own fearlessness anymore. Her long tangled hair was around the halfway point in the transition stage to dreads and was carelessly pulled back into a ponytail and tucked into her helmet. Her legs looked like they were attempting to grow dreads as well, as they hadn't been shaved in months and rivaled my brother's. I remember stifling my laughter as I watched her raise her arms to demonstrate a paddle technique and noticed the hair under her pits matched her legs, perhaps an attempt to outwardly celebrate her fearlessness, her adventurous spirit, her campaign for sucking the marrow out of life that probably brought her here to this small mountain town to conquer her fears and insecurities. As we prepared to climb into the raft and set out along the daunting rapids, she offered her last set of instructions.

"If you fall out," she advised, "whatever you do, don't fight the current. If you fight, you will drown. Don't grab on to anything, don't waste your energy trying to swim. Just relax and let go. Put your body into this position." She paused and stretched her legs out into a yogalike stance and curled her hands around her neck. "Then let the current guide you. Someone will help you, but the best chance you have of surviving is to let go and follow the flow of the current." For some reason, I never forgot that advice. It was enough, at least, to settle me into a place where I let go of my fear of falling out and drowning and instead chose to enjoy the thrill and thrashing that crazy half hour of being thrust along the current granted us.

I enjoyed the summer of 2010 with its beach picnics, evening family walks, and backyard bonfires just as I enjoyed that wild and crazy white-water rafting experience. I let go. And on July 1, Brett and I celebrated our fourth wedding anniversary. Tradition has it that every year on our anniversary, we head back to DaRuMa, the Japanese steakhouse where, years beforehand, I nervously fumbled with my water glass and self-consciously regretted my little-bit-of-cleavage-baring shirt on our first official just-the-two-of-us date. It's always grand and romantic to go back, to sit in that same booth and reminisce about how far we've come and where we're going. I usually have one too many beers—which feels good—and by the end of our dinner I'm all tipsy and sentimental, leaning in too close, talking too loud, and getting overly excited about future plans.

"Let's have more babies," I'll say. "Let's go camping more. Let's have neighbors over for dinner. Let's plan a trip to Colorado." And it doesn't matter if we really do them all or not (good thing, because I once suggested "let's get tattoos right now"). Something about saying it out loud with a nice buzz on our anniversary while Brett is patiently smiling and telling me, "Sure, let's do all those things," feels like a meaningful rite of passage. It's a bonding experience in the same kind of way dancing to "Y.M.C.A." with your cousins after a shot of tequila at your wedding reception makes you wish they all lived next door. And you tell them that. Repeatedly.

I was feeling the same kind of high-on-life enthusiasm that July 1, but for some reason, I craved something different than our traditional night of chopsticking shrimp and ginger-soaked beef at DaRuMa. My new flow-with-the-current-and-let-go mantra wasn't really complemented with dressing up and doing the same thing we'd been doing for years. I wanted something fresh, something more laid-back, something that represented my shift in perspective.

"Let's find a dive bar," I suggested to Brett as I spritzed perfume and dug through my closet for some anniversary-ish dress. My dad and Gary were in town and were headed over to watch the kids, and Brett and I relished the opportunity to spend a little more time getting ready for a rare date, just the two of us.

Brett looked pleasantly surprised. "Really? But you're Tradition Girl. You love traditions. You sure you want to break it this year?" He was being sweet, really, because I knew inside he was thrilled I'd suggest a dive bar, which matched his laid-back, baseball cap, flip-flop-wearin' heart.

"Yeah, I'm sure. I just want to relax tonight. I want to wear jeans, eat something fried, and drink freezing cold beer belly-up at the bar. Do you mind?"

"Not at all," he answered, less enthusiastic, of course, than I knew he was feeling.

So I traded an anniversary-ish dress for the comfort of blue jeans—balancing the laid-back look with festive heels to make up for it—and to the bar we headed to celebrate the glorious day we promised "for better or for worse." Those words seemed to echo the reality that the last four years had brought full circle that night. We dangled our feet from high bar stools, side by side, and listened to loud music from the performing garage band while we tipped back cold beer and ate cheesy, deep-fried things we wouldn't normally indulge in. It was very much a riding-with-the-current night, and it felt entirely wonderful to let go and enjoy the carefree energy the summer was lavishly ladling upon us.

On the way home, we passed the church where we were married, vacant that late and enchantingly lit up by a smattering of street-lights. Brett gave me one of those are-you-thinking-what-I'm-thinking glances, I smiled, and one U-turn later, we were pulling onto the sacred ground of the North Naples United Methodist Church parking lot. We scrunched together in front of the Village Chapel sign and stretched our

arms out with the camera for an awkward self-portrait, and I joked that it felt a little strange being slightly intoxicated standing on God's premises. And the crazy thing about the entire night was that, for all the epic life conversations we had ever had on this memorable night when we looked back and foresaw the future, I don't think Down syndrome came up one time. No third-beer revelation where I'm all, "Dude, what the hell just happened to us this year?" or "How are we going to do this?" No alcohol-induced sudden breakdowns. Just a high-on-life husband and wife who—four years, two babies, and a whole heck of a lot of good times ago—stood on this very same ground after a memorable "I do."

We were riding the steady current and enjoying the satisfaction of another anniversary under our belt. Later, we pulled into the driveway and tiptoed in the house—so as not to wake the babies—and found them both awake, all jammied up, waiting for our return. We hugged and kissed and caved into Lainey's plea to light a candle, cement it into a cookie, and sing "Happy Anniversary to You."

And it really did feel like we were easily flowing through the current—the best part, the smooth part, the water that glides against slippery river rocks and swirls in gentle circles. The ease with which we flowed that summer restored us, and it's a good thing, because there were rapids ahead.

jeremy

A WEEK AFTER OUR ANNIVERSARY, WE DECIDED
to take our first real family vacation since Lainey was born. Plan
was, we would join my dad and Gary for four days in Key West,
leave our mundane routines behind, watch sunsets on Mallory
Square, and stay up late telling stories on our hotel balcony.
I was more than psyched for our trip, and the day before we
left, I had everything ready. Cute bathing suits packed, camera batteries charged, and backpacks stocked with salty pret-
zels and granola bars to help make the six-hour drive across
Alligator Alley and down-the-island skip to the Keys a little
easier.

I get a little high on life right before vacations. I don't know,
maybe it's the brewing excitement of getting away, the rare opportunity of shaving off the responsibilities of reality and focusing entirely on what matters most. Whatever the case, I get
sentimental. The night before we left, I hardly slept. Instead I
lay awake in bed thinking about my place in the world, what I
was grateful for, how far we'd come. I finally decided to get up

and do something about it, right before the sun awakened the eager members of my household who couldn't wait to hit the road. When I think hard, I write hard. So I hit the computer at 6:00 A.M. with a hot cup of coffee and a weakened filter for what was appropriate to write and what wasn't.

I wrote fast and furious that morning, titling my blog post "On Down Syndrome" and rattling off how happy I was despite the fact that I had had "a moment" that week wondering if the way Nella repeatedly shook a toy was some sort of Down syndrome side effect. My goal? To honestly express my fears and low moments and yet remind myself of just how insignificant Down syndrome was in the grand scheme of life and its little pleasures. My result? Internet Social Disaster.

We had just arrived in Key West when I realized the post I wrote that morning had become a lively source of comments, many of them negative. I had had negative feedback before, sure, but this time it seemed like an uproar. Again, some couldn't understand my okayness with it all and suggested I was in deep denial. One comment actually said something to the effect of "If her shaking a toy made you upset, you just wait. It's going to get so much worse. When your kid is made fun of and you're at the hospital every day, maybe you'll pull yourself out of denial and realize what this life really is." And more comments came. Soon, the quiet space of my post's comment board became a boxing ring. An uppercut: "You're in denial, honey." A jab back: "I agree wholeheartedly. Lay off her." And it wouldn't stop. I should have turned the computer off and walked away, but I was strangely drawn to the drama.

The sad thing is that the bulk of the response to what I wrote was good and assuring—like-minded sentiments from parents much fur-

ther down this journey who were celebrating life much like we were. But I let the fraction of negativity affect me. I began to mercilessly question myself—on vacation, when I should have been sipping mai tais and reading John Grisham's latest. I wondered again, based on a few comments, if maybe I had it all wrong. And I let it consume me to the point of sobbing phone conversations with my sister, my friends, anyone who would tell me, "No, no, they have it all wrong." And while I am sorry to say I let a few people I don't even know who share the right to a different viewpoint get me down, I am glad I had that moment. It was needful, like getting dumped at your junior prom is needful in teaching a heartbroken girl that her happiness does not lie in the hands of a prepubescent, squeaky-voiced kid with a rented tux and bad skin. Not that it makes getting dumped any easier.

"Babe, you have to let this go," Brett finally told me from the ledge of the hot tub as he watched me silently sulk in thought amid a sea of swirling bubbles on Day Two of our vacation. "We believe in our approach and we know it works for our family. We know God blessed us with these beautiful children, and we have no idea what the future holds. You're going to let a few people take that away from you?"

I felt silly and ashamed. He was incredibly right, and I was incredibly immature for considering disposing of a beautiful outlook that had taken thirty-one years of both good and bad experiences to chisel into what it had become. It was mine, and I needed to step up to the plate and own it.

The great thing about having this sort of breakdown in Key West is that the message I needed to hear—to own my celebratory feelings and wear them with confidence—is literally broadcasted from every inch

of signage in the colorful town that proudly refers to itself as "One Human Family." And, by Day Three, I was beginning to feel a new confidence settle in as our family walked to breakfast, holding hands, passing the random herd of chickens that *bawk*ed their way across the streets they owned and the Hemingway cats that purred contentedly from shop steps. That morning I counted the growing list of signs that spoke to me. A small carved plaque, lopsidedly hung from a resident's front door: LOOK FOR THE GOOD, it said. A flashy lime bumper sticker, taped to the back of an old rusted beater: LIFE IS GOOD, it proclaimed. A large printed banner, raised high above a storefront: DARE TO BE DIFFERENT, it declared. I've never been one to trade my way of thinking due to a saying on a bumper sticker and I, to this day, have never honked for loving Jesus, but I will say my teetering confidence was strengthened something fierce that week, thanks to a much needed mental boot camp that happened to include some blatant truths displayed in the many artful signs and stickers of Key West.

I borrowed my new mantra from the great words of William Shakespeare—"To thine own self be true"—and came home from Key West with a faint tan and a new fearlessness, not only for expressing what I felt deep in my bones, but for facing the unknown of where life's current would take us. The only thing that mattered—and I knew this—was the very moment we were blessed to be living. The *right now*.

THAT *RIGHT NOW* HAPPENED TO BE THE CELEBRATION of half a year along our new journey when we returned home from vacation, and I knew what it meant. The first check off the medical to-do list Dr. Foley had written on that small piece of paper she had handed me months before—the one that was crumpled and hidden under coupons taped to my fridge. Six months meant another checkup, an eye exam, and a few blood tests that included a CBC (Complete Blood Count) and a thyroid screen.

A week before Nella's scheduled appointment, I noticed a spot on her right forearm. It was a small bruise, no bigger than a dime, and made up of tiny red dots or *petechiae,* as the medical books call them. My heart sank. Just a few weeks earlier I had read a story of a one-year-old little girl with Down syndrome who was diagnosed with leukemia, and it all started when her mom noticed—yup, you guessed it—a patch of petechiae on her arm.

It was my biggest fear—the first "added concern" I had read about months earlier, the one that hit hard when I first discovered its possibility and then gravely loomed in my brain. I wanted to tell Brett about it—to point out the bruise and tell him everything I knew about petechia and leukemia and children with Down syndrome. I wanted to fall in a heap on the floor and scream, "No," but I also didn't want to say it out loud. Because then, maybe, it would be true. So I said nothing, letting Fear back into my brain where it set up Command Central and then stretched itself all the way down to my stomach where it knotted and grew.

Without causing too much alarm, I called Dr. Foley's office to see if I could get our blood work done before our appointment. "That would be much less of a hassle," is, as I recall, how I worded it. "I'm *this* close

to losing my mind" seemed a little too dramatic. She called a script for the CBC and our thyroid screen over to the hospital, and I was there the next morning with Nella and Fear in tow. As if being scared and anxious wasn't enough, the blood draw pretty much turned out to be the experience from hell. Oh, it was awful. The nurses, God bless them, did everything they could, but they couldn't find a vein. My girl screamed and cried as they stuck her arms, her hands, her feet, and I laid my entire body over her tiny self and whispered "Oh, baby, Mama's here" a million times. My tears dripped into her tears, her eyes met mine, and together we were one hot mess. An hour later, two tiny vials were filled, and I carried my exhausted girl home to wait for the results.

I tried to forget about it, I did. And I really, truly think I convinced myself that I was being silly and this was nothing. I had had these moments before in motherhood, and they had always turned out fine. So I relaxed that night, even taking my friends Suzanne and Wylie up on their offer to meet for a drink. Brett encouraged me to go, perhaps tuning into that magical spousal gift of sensing when something's not right and you need your girlfriends, and I relinquished the nighttime routine duties and headed up to the small plaza bar where they were waiting for me. I felt good—calm, untroubled, eager to talk about unimportant things and replenish the liveliness I had lost earlier that day.

I regained my liveliness in no time. We sat at the bar, eating mozzarella sticks, telling stories that made us clutch our sides and slap the table. Wylie has the best laugh—it's loud and raspy and when it comes, it comes full force, maximum volume with a wide smile and enunciated *ha-ha-has* that turn heads and lighten moods. We called Heidi, who was in Michigan, from the bar and hollered "Wish you were here!" and "We're having so much fun!" obnoxiously into the phone like high school girls at a sleepover. And I almost forgot about petechiae and blood tests until one of the girls asked me what I did that day.

I answered cautiously, blundering my words, fumbling with my drink. "Oh, Nella had a blood test this morning that took forever, and it really sucked."

"But everything's okay, right? It's just standard?" Suzanne studied my face for a glint of concern.

"Yeah, it's just—" I stopped. I couldn't fake it. I looked up and noticed a rough-looking beefy man in a stained T-shirt across the bar from us, probably on his tenth beer, staring at my eyes now welling with tears. He gave me one of those "Honey, I don't know what your problem is but I'm sorry your life is shitty" looks and nodded his condolences.

And I lost it. I cried right there at the bar and told them everything—the little bruise that scared the hell out of me and the awful blood test and the fact that I was pretending not to think about it but that, yes, I had knots in my stomach and it was all I could do not to run home and pull her out of her crib and hold her close until I knew. I rattled every bit of it off without stopping to take a breath and when I finished, I wiped the tears off my cheek with the back of my hand, smeared under my eyes to clean up any mascara remains, and laughed. Because I was, after all, sitting at a bar having a therapy session with not just Suzanne and Wylie but everyone gathered at that semicircular table that curled around and united us all.

Wylie raised her hand and signaled the bartender. "Um, we need a beer, right here, right now," she demanded, pointing at my empty glass and flashing one of those "You should have noticed" glances. Like "Dude, seriously, she's a mess. A little help here." Within seconds he slammed a frosty brew in front of me and a bowl of lime wedges followed.

"I'm fine, I'm fine," I laughed. "I didn't realize it was festering like this. I know it will be okay, I really do. It's just that it really sucks. It sucks a mother even has to think about this."

The girls pulled their stools closer and leaned in, driven by some strange force that gave them the ability to say the perfect things at the perfect time. They listened, they cried, they laughed. And it all blended together for the Amazing Bar Bear Hug of 2010.

"I don't know if this makes you feel better," Suzanne finally offered, "but I thought I'd share that Jon had a nightmare in the middle of the night last night and he bit me in his sleep. Hard. Look." She held up her

hand and proudly pointed out her husband's teeth indentations, scarred under her left thumb.

And that did it. Another round of laughter, Wylie's leading loud and recognizable among the rest. But it was good—that moment of healing that swept the fears and brushed them to the side, still present, but manageable. The Net had caught me once again, there when I needed them, strong when I was not.

I went home with less of a knot and more of an appreciation for my friends that night—the ones who had continued to rise to the occasion without even knowing it that year. Dr. Foley's office manager called the next day to let us know the CBC came back normal and, by the end of the night, you couldn't even see the tiny bruise that started all this. But somewhere within me, I knew it wouldn't be the last time I waited anxiously for results or cried at a bar about how scared I was and expressed just how much I'd be lost without my kids. It is a rite of passage not just for special needs, but for motherhood—to worry, to cry, to go to the awful place of "what would I do IF?" We ache when they ache, and we writhe with distress at the thought that they will, at some point in life, be hurt. And they will. Our children will hurt, many times along our journey, and there's nothing we can do about it but love them and hold them and whisper in their ears, "Oh, baby, Mama's here." And when that time comes, we need Suzannes and Wylies and Heidis. We need sisters and brothers, moms and dads, cousins and friends. Hell, we need beefy guys

in bars who offer condolences with drunk eyes. We take what we can get
and hold on to it like driftwood escaped from a shipwreck. It holds us
up, keeps us afloat, sustains the only breath we have left until we get to
dry land. And I'm thankful for that—*for them*.

A week later I'd need my friends again. I took Nella for her six-month
eye exam, completely assured her eyes were fine, and was taken off guard
when the doctor concluded our lengthy appointment with a nonchalant
"So, she needs glasses," like it was no big deal. He might as well have
just said she had a hangnail. And I knew it was no big deal. God, compared to cancer or the hundred other things I could be worried about,
this was definitely nothing, and I'd be silly to get upset. But I'm still a
mama—a mama who's memorized the sweet face of my almond-eyed one
so meticulously, I can trace her cheeks in my sleep. So it took me a couple
swallows and blinks before I got there.

I worked hard to keep my tears at bay in that office, but by the time I hit
the parking lot, I was using one hand to shield the sun from Nella's dilated
pupils and the other to dial my friend Meg. Meg doesn't have kids and may
not know what to say from a mom's perspective, but she's glamorous and
fashionable and I knew if anyone could make me feel better about a baby
looking cute wearing specs, it was Meg. She did just that. After a tearful phone conversation with her in the car on the way home, I no sooner
checked my e-mail when I got home to find one from her titled "I mean,
come on" and in it a bulleted list of links to cute kids with glasses. Like

Meg Ryan's kid sporting delicate red frames, Dakota Fanning's little sister rocking out a pair of wire rims, or, as Meg put it, "that cute as shit kid from *Jerry Maguire*" who, as we all know, rocked out glasses like nobody's business. The e-mail ended with HELL YEAH . . . in all caps.

So I decided we'd make the best of our baby having to wear glasses. I'd find cute frames and if I couldn't find them, I'd bend titanium and make them. Thankfully, an Internet search for the smallest rectangular frames I could find and a chocolate brown paint job later, we had the cutest damn bespectacled baby you'd ever seen. Nella soon earned the name "The Professor," and I couldn't get enough of her soulful round eyes staring out at me past the smart little wall of tiny painted frames. Turns out a second opinion a few months later would scratch the hassle of baby glasses altogether, but still, the experience added another notch to our ever-growing belt of learning to make the best of things.

As crazy as the current had flowed that month—with my hot-button blog post, the leukemia scare, the debut of our little professor—it was still just a small whirlpool leading up to the most significant turning point for me since Nella was born.

Wrapping your brain around the concept of your child having Down syndrome is a long series of steps. It began for me with concentrated grief that hit hard and sudden when I first saw that my baby's eyes looked different, but it eventually smoothed to such a comforting place of love and acceptance when I realized she was just a baby—*our* baby—and not much different from any other baby. You read things in the beginning to cope, and you talk to other parents and look at pictures of other kids with almond eyes. You listen to your pediatrician, you let your friends help you, and you arrive at a comfortable place of being okay with everything. But, for most of us embarking upon our new journey, there is still an unsettling feeling that comes with imagining your child grown up. Because Down syndrome looks a lot different at thirty than it does at six months.

I didn't want to go there yet—wasn't sure if I was ready, but I knew it was inevitable, especially when I realized the National Down Syndrome

Congress's 2010 convention was being held in Orlando, just three and a half hours away from us. It was a painful decision to go and in the preceding weeks, I dwelled in a confusing place of wanting to force myself to do something uncomfortable and yet, at the same time, pulling back, reminding myself it was perfectly acceptable to stay home and enjoy the baby stage—that I didn't have to prove anything to anyone, not even myself. And then I'd challenge myself again. *What, are you scared? Can't you handle it? This is your life.* But I *was* scared.

"I have to go," I told Brett one night. "I don't have a choice. This is our life, Brett. It won't be easy, but it will be good. And what are the chances it happens to be in Orlando just six months after we gave birth? Seriously, Brett. It's a sign, right?"

"You do whatever you want to do," he answered predictably. "But don't do it for anyone but yourself if you're going to go. You don't *have* to go, babe, and there's nothing wrong with staying home and going some other year if that's what you want to do."

I was confused and overwhelmed and couldn't make up my mind. Once a year, thousands of families of children with Down syndrome come together in one place. All different ages, all different capabilities. For one weekend, they sit in lectures, join together at banquets, celebrate at dances, and feel united. Was I ready to be in that place? Was I ready to face the future so suddenly?

A little catalyst came when I learned I would be winning a media award for my account of our journey on my blog. I cried when I got the call. I was surprised, yes, but more than that, I was so entirely grateful that what I was writing about was doing something good beyond my own healing—that being true to myself and expressing honestly the feelings on this new journey was helping other people too. And to be recognized for that was incredibly satisfying and humbling. Perhaps another sign as well, I thought. But I still wasn't convinced. In a moment of lost clarity, I called up a number I found online for the NDSC and lost my mind to the first person who answered the phone. Bless his heart. I'm embarrassed to this day for what I put that poor unsuspecting man through. As soon as he answered, my voice cracked and wavered. And something to the effect of "Hi, David, this is Kelle Hampton, and I'm scared to come to the convention" came out, except typed words cannot do justice to just how pathetic it sounded. I became a child, crying and grasping at anything that would make me feel better. I think I asked him if he had a child with Down syndrome and if he was scared too. God, I could have asked him if he believed in Santa Claus for all I know, but I do know he was kind and reassuring and made me feel very welcome to attend that convention but very accepted if I didn't.

We decided Brett would hold down the fort with Lainey and the boys, and I would go to the convention with Nella and a few friends. And yes, I was scared. But I was also hopeful. You have to work your muscles to become stronger, and I knew that weekend would work weak muscles that were begging to become strong.

Heidi had offered to fly down from her summer in Michigan to go with me, but I couldn't possibly have asked her for any more after all she had been to me that year. A few other friends were coming along—Katie, Stephanie, and Marsha—and the idea of being present with girlfriends at a nice hotel in Orlando—with hot tubs and water slides and a lobby coffee shop—nicely balanced my anxiety about being at the convention.

I didn't know what to expect, so I made things up just to prepare myself. I pictured being in a giant room, gathered in a circle with hundreds of adults with Down syndrome. I imagined individuals who spoke differently, looked differently, acted differently. I figured I might naturally feel sorry for them, and I didn't want to. I foresaw myself holding my girl, looking out into the crowd and picturing every one of them as Nella, and I expected that moment of realization—that second of connection—would be painful and hard to bear. We talked about it on the three-and-a-half-hour drive up to Orlando. We talked about what it would look like and how it would feel.

"It's gonna be okay," I'd say with a smile, leaning forward from the backseat with Katie to form a conversation huddle between Marsha and Stephanie up front. "It's gonna be good for me." Sometimes when I'm scared, I adopt mantras and "It's gonna be okay" had seemed to do the job pretty well for the past six months.

"What are you most nervous about?" Stephanie asked.

I thought a minute and formed an answer. "I'm afraid of seeing people who can't do what I want Nella to do, and that it will make me very sad."

"It's okay to be sad," Steph answered.

"I hate being sad," I replied.

Katie piped up. "I think it's going to be awesome. I think you're going to leave happy. I think we're going to have a blast and everyone in that room is going to make you laugh and smile and be excited for the future."

I nodded. "I hope so." And, without saying a word, Katie reached her hand over and squeezed mine.

And so we drove and laughed and listened to music. We stopped at 7-Eleven and ran in to get sodas and Corn Nuts and Twizzlers. We took our shoes off, danced in the backseat, hand-signaled for truckers to honk, and cheered when they did. It was the perfect mix of a journey to face my fears with a touch of senior-year spring break to ease the anxiety.

As soon as we settled into our hotel, we began getting ready for the convention banquet that evening. We traded earrings, helped each other pick out shoes, and shared hair dryers as we made small talk. I whipped out some *Risky Business* dance moves in my underwear while I primed in the mirror, and I'm pretty sure someone took a picture of it, but the point is, it was all obviously an attempt to calm nerves, and it was working. We had planned, before the banquet, to visit a family from Delaware I had been e-mailing

with for the past few weeks. Rick and Amy were attending the convention with their four-year-old daughter, Kayla, who had Down syndrome, and Amy had invited all of us to join them in their hotel suite an hour before the festivities began.

I'll never forget knocking on their suite door. I was nervous, not only to meet them and their daughter, but for the evening that would follow. I was nervous for the banquet, for possibly having to say something when I accepted my award, for facing the pain of looking into the future. But it all melted the moment the door of Rick and Amy's suite creaked open and a beautiful, blond, vivacious woman met my fear with a warm smile and a hug that tightly enveloped me with strength.

"Aahhhhh! I've been waiting forever to get my hands on this baby!" Amy shrieked as she reached out and scooped Nella out of my arms. "Come on in and make yourselves at home!" Amy motioned for us to get comfortable on the couches and called for her daughter to come say hello. "Kayla, this is Baby Nella. Remember the baby we saw on the computer? This is her! And this is Kelle."

Kayla looked up at me with wild blue eyes and smiled. "Hi, Kelle," she said. And then, after each introduction, she repeated everyone's name. As clear as day. As beautiful as ever. "Hi, Stephanie; Hi, Katie; Hi, Marsha." And I wept. Hot tears rolled down my cheeks as I watched this beautiful little girl touch my baby's cheeks, whispering, "She's so cute," and looking to her mama for approval.

"She *is* cute, isn't she?" Amy answered, stroking Kayla's long blond hair, so proud, so completely aware that I was comforted by her love and awareness.

It felt like we had met long-lost friends that evening as we sank into those couches and talked about babies and friends and growing stronger. It didn't last very long, but I will always remember it. And then Kayla read to us. She read big words like *spaghetti* and *school* and *mother* from large flash cards Amy had made from poster board. And all I could do was smile and cry and whisper to Amy over and over, "You don't know what this means. You have no idea how healing this is." Kayla

grabbed Stephanie's hand and said "Let's go play," and two seconds later we found them in the bathroom—Stephanie sitting cross-legged on the floor laughing while Kayla, dressed in her polka-dot party dress, rattled commands from inside the bathtub-turned-boat.

I couldn't stop crying beautiful, happy tears. And soon, it was time to walk to the banquet room of the Coronado Springs Hotel for the main event.

"Let's go," I announced. "I'm not afraid." And I wasn't.

I had felt this surge of confidence before in life. I don't know why I doubted if it would come because it always does when I need it. When I turned twenty-one, I went skydiving. I was terrified, even completely regretting that I told my dad it's what I wanted for my birthday as we drove an hour from our vacation hotel in Florida out to Lake Okeechobee for the experience that warm, still morning. But I wanted to prove to myself I was a badass. So my mouth kept quiet every time my brain begged it to speak up and back out. There is the moment the plane takes off, when you swear you're peeing in your dive suit and your stomach is knotted with so much fear you're sure you're going to vomit. And there is the moment where your palms are sweating and your legs are shaking and you're just about to tell the guy strapped to your back that you changed your mind. But then there is the moment the door opens. And all you see is clouds. You hear the deafening rumble of the plane engine and feel the void of open air that calls you. And you close your eyes and feel it. You feel the fear settling, replaced by the thrill of courage. It is . . . *amazing*. And when the guy strapped to your back taps your elbow that it's a go, you smile and hang on. Because you are ready.

THE MOMENT AMY OPENED THE DOOR TO ESCORT US ALL to the banquet was exactly like the moment I gripped the doorway of the small prop plane that launched me into the skies over Lake Okeechobee ten years earlier. I held my girl close to my chest and smiled. Because I was ready. And as we walked, I watched as families paraded from their rooms to join us. Adults. With Down syndrome. Teenagers, children, brothers, sisters. I had been so scared of this moment, and here I was, proudly clutching my girl and feeling the thrill of courage, the surge of love.

"Are you okay?" Stephanie whispered as we walked.

"I'm great," I answered. "I'm so glad I came."

We were almost to the entrance of the banquet room when I saw them walking. An older couple, hand in hand. And, as they got closer, I noticed they had Down syndrome but forgot just as soon as I had noticed. When they saw Nella, they ran to meet us.

"Baby," the man said softly, reaching out to touch her fingers.

"We love babies," the woman replied. And they stood there, the man and the woman who happened to have Down syndrome—the ones who loved each other—cooing to my girl, holding her hand, and I wept and smiled and said "Thank you." I watched as Nella looked into their eyes, as they soothed her with their gentle touch, their calm fuss over how tiny she was, how pretty she was. And it felt like I was soaring. And just like that, they rejoined hands and walked ahead of us into the hallway.

"I'm so glad I came," I said again to Katie.

"I know you are." She smiled. "I am too."

We walked into the ballroom of the Coronado Springs Resort and were met with a lively energy you could almost touch. The place was buzzing with people and laughter and happiness. There were hundreds

of families here to celebrate, and I felt like I belonged. As the ceremony commenced after we found our seats, I held a sleeping Nella in one arm and picked at my salad with another, all the while feeling peace. I didn't know what I was going to say when I walked to the stage to accept our award, but something came out—something honest I hadn't even thought about before I said it. I told everyone in that room that I was scared to come. I told them I was so sorry for not wanting to be on this journey with them just months earlier. I told them it was hard to be welcomed in the beginning, hard to hear things like "welcome to the family" and "welcome to the club" because I didn't ask to be there. Because I didn't think I wanted to be there. But then I cried and told them I was thankful I was there. That, for the first time, I was proud to be part of their family, and that there was nowhere I would have rather been that night. As I walked off the stage with my girl, a blubbering mess, I remember two things. One, the kind man named David who helped me down the steps and told me he was the one who took my call the day I embarrassingly needed some anonymous therapy (and I thought I'd never have to face him). And two, the young man who walked from the back of the ballroom, zigzagging through tables to come see us. He was in his twenties, perhaps, and he had Down syndrome. I waited while he finally made his way to us. And then he hugged me tight, Nella squished between us, and said, "You peech touch my hawt." He repeated it over and over, tapping his heart with one hand, stroking Nella's fingers with the other until I realized what he was saying. *Your speech touched my heart.* And I felt so much love.

The night went on as I surrendered myself to the emotion present in

that place. There was the crazy fun energy like that of a wedding reception, and there was healing and hope and an amazing sense of community. But mostly, there was love. Possibly more love present in that room
than any other place in the world on that very night.

My favorite moment of the night was a brief meeting I shared in the
hallway. I had slipped out with Nella during the event to change her in
the bathroom and when I emerged into the hallway to head back into the
ballroom, there was a handsome man standing by the ballroom door.
He had been waiting for us. He too had a magic chromosome and smiled
with almond eyes at Nella. He reached his hand out to shake mine.

"I'm Jhay-a-mee," he said.

"Hi, Jeremy." I smiled and stretched my hand out to take his.

He looked at Nella and stroked her leg. "She's beau-i-ful," he whispered.

"Thank you," I answered, still holding his one hand and doing my
best to repress my tears.

Then he took my hand into his and said, "I'm sorry."

My throat tightened as I searched for words. He heard my speech. He
was apologizing for my pain—for my pain of having a child who bears
the same chromosome he does. He thinks I didn't want a baby like him.
I held Nella tight in one arm and squeezed his hand tighter in the other.

"No, Jeremy, it's okay."

"I'm sorry foh you hawt. I'm sorry you sad," he said, and he placed his
hand above my heart and smiled. "She's so beau-i-ful," he said again,
smiling.

And all I could do was stand there, crying, holding Jeremy's hand,
whispering "Thank you, thank you" over and over. "Jeremy, I'm okay
now. I'm happy. I love her so much." I stopped and watched as my tears
fell onto Nella, and I squeezed Jeremy's hand again. "I'm so sorry I was
sad at first. But it's okay. I just didn't know. But now I know . . . *I'm lucky.*"

And he knew. I know he knew I was lucky and that I was okay. It was
all I could do not to run back into the ballroom, find poor David in the
crowd, and make him give me another therapy session, but I didn't. I

was so ashamed. I felt so small in the presence of this lovely man who knew I had grieved the connection my child had to him and, at that moment, I felt like Jeremy was far wiser than me. I should be the one apologizing. I wanted to take it all back—my words, my feelings, my regret from the moment my girl was placed in my arms. And yet, I felt Jeremy understood it all—like he knew it was part of the journey, and he sympathized with me. He told me he understood—with his eyes, with his words, with the way he held my hand and stroked my girl's sweet cheeks.

I thanked Jeremy, hugged him, and told myself I'd never forget that moment. I walked back into that room and celebrated life with the hundreds of beautiful souls present. I clapped at the end of every speech and passed Nella to new friends at our table who were aching to hold her. As soon as the ceremony was over, throngs of effervescent personalities overtook the room, preparing for the dance that was to follow. A teenage girl with green glasses that matched her green almond eyes told me she had to get to the dance because she and her boyfriend were going to be cuttin' loose on the floor.

"We'll see about that," her mom muttered, rolling her eyes and smiling as her daughter dragged her toward the party.

The girls and I had plans for a fondue dessert at a nearby restaurant, but before we left, I hugged as many bodies as I could find. I had done it. I had faced my fears, I had made the jump, and it felt good.

Before I left, I grabbed my phone, took a picture of Kayla, and sent it to Brett with a text: *This is our beautiful future. Tonight was really good, babe. Better than I could have ever imagined.*

And it was.

nella's
rockstars

I CAME HOME FROM THE CONVENTION WITH NEW
hope and, I have to admit, a sense of pride. I surprised myself.
Ninety percent of the thrill of skydiving isn't so much in the act
itself but in the satisfaction of saying "I went skydiving" afterward—even if it's only to yourself. And though, yes, the convention turned out to be an inspiring event, it was what it did for
me afterward that fueled me. Not only did it give me that "I did
it" satisfaction, but it allowed me to purposely pick the Publix
check-out lane where the woman with Down syndrome bags
groceries. It allowed me to stop feeling sorry for her and finally
look her in the eyes and think of Jeremy. It allowed me to smile
and tell her I liked her charm bracelet or even fast-forward
thirty years and imagine my daughter grown up, just like her,
and peacefully accept what it might look like. I ripped the Band-
Aid off, and it wasn't so bad.

The thing is, we don't really know what the future looks like.
And that thought takes my breath away just as much as it calms
me into a place where I am forced to enjoy this very moment.

Part of facing your fears is going there. You have to go there—to the deepest pain of what you fear. You have to feel it—to hold the hot potato of hurt and know that even if life takes you to that place, you will get through it. And knowing that not only allows you to let the fear go but it fuels you with a passion to make the best out of what you have, to grab the reins and purposefully steer yourself where you want to go.

I realized when I returned from the convention that I had also proved myself wrong. The day after Nella was born, a small pile of informative pamphlets and support group brochures began growing at the end of my hospital bed, and I hated it. There were photos of families at Buddy Walks—the national campaign that organizes walks all over the country for families with Down syndrome—handouts for local groups, forms for receiving services. Back then, I didn't want to be a part of anything—no support groups, no Buddy Walks, no conventions. I wanted to go home with my baby, do it our own way, and I wanted everyone in that hospital room to know this was the way it was going to be.

"Just so y'all know," I declared all Rocky-faced and puffy-eyed to everyone in the room that day, "I'm not going to be doing the Buddy Walk thing, I'm not starting a club, and I'm not going to a support group. I just want to move on. Okay?" They all nodded their heads and smiled because they knew my head would spin if they didn't, but I'm sure they recognized my declaration as grief-stricken words masking a hurting heart. In fact, even writing about those early days is like writing about a girl I once knew a long time ago, and I will always be so sad for her.

Pain has a way of pulling you forward to a surprising place of "I didn't know I had it in me," and while you think there is no way you will ever make it through in the beginning, you do. Going to the convention may have blessed me with a new fearlessness, but I think the confidence was there all along—hidden deep within me like a seed under cold, frozen ground. It was very much alive, just quiet and unrecognized until the right elements were present to force it to bloom. And when it did? Well, if you give a mouse a cookie, he might just ask for a glass of milk. And if you conquer a fear you didn't think you'd overcome, you might just think you're a rockstar. I wanted to know what else I was capable of, and I was determined to rock the hell out of whatever it was.

SHORTLY AFTER I RETURNED HOME FROM THE CONVENTION, I did two crazy things. First, I bought three plane tickets to Montana. I had corresponded so much with my blog friend Nici, and our friendship had grown so beautifully since Nella was born, that it was time I took my girls across the country to meet her face-to-face. Second, I googled to find a nearby Buddy Walk and, crazy as it was, discovered Naples was having its very first one in October. So I signed up that very same day and sent out a mass e-mail to everyone we knew inviting them to come. Suddenly, I was fueled with a "Go Big or Go Home" attitude. And it felt amazing.

I'm still a little shocked that Brett was okay with me taking the girls on a one-week continental jaunt to visit someone I had never met, but I think he knew it was important. Meeting, by chance, this person who was so different from me and yet felt so connected to my life was one of the greatest perks that came with starting my blog a few years before, and I wanted to take this crazy experience to the friendship version of second base. Besides, it was a fearless thing to do, and I wanted more fearlessness in my life. I wanted to act on hunches and have faith in myself. I wanted to do some big things with my one wild and precious life.

And so it was: we woke up at 6:00 A.M. on a September morning, buckled sleepy girls into car seats, heaved heavy suitcases into the trunk, and hauled across Alligator Alley to the Fort Lauderdale airport where Brett kissed us good-bye and made us promise to text and call throughout the trip. I felt far more put together than usual—almost arrogantly so—because I was so proud of the way I pulled a suitcase, pushed a stroller, jiggled a baby, and balanced a camera, a laptop, a cell phone, and three boarding passes all at once that I actually had to consciously tell myself to wipe the "Hey, look at me, I'm doing it!" expression off my face. Actually, it took seeing a mom wearing spiked heels and leather pants, pushing a twin stroller and holding a toddler's hand that did it for me. Because I may have made it across the country alone with two kids but I sure as hell didn't look that good doing it. I wore my ugly shoes for comfort and my scarf was wet from rinsing it in the airport sink after the fringe dragged in the toilet. But hey, I did it.

I was so caught up in my satisfaction of our trip going so swimmingly that I almost forgot my kids and I would be spending a week with someone I'd never really physically connected with. And what if, on Day Two, it was a total bust and I wanted to go home? What if we bored each other and I dragged my girls across the country for nothing? Or worse, what if she was crazy?

Two hours later, my fears melted when I stepped off the plane into a small terminal in the Missoula airport that, with its knotty pine accents and large framed pictures of forests and bears and mountains, felt welcoming in that ski lodge family vacation kind of way. I strapped Nella into her sling and held tightly to Lainey's hand as we gathered our things and hesitantly searched the hallway for a familiar face.

And then I saw her standing there, just as hesitant, her wild curls pulled loosely into two twirly buns and artsy strings of turquoise beads dangling from her ears, distinguishing her as the free, creative Missoulian I had come to love through words and chats. Our eyes met and all reluctance dissolved.

Just as the mountains had me at hello, so did my friend I'd never met. I knew there in the middle of the airport as we hugged and cried and barricaded the exiting passenger route for a good minute or so that our week was going to be just fine. I knew as she grabbed Nella and I hoisted suitcases into the back of her car, which was littered with garbage she didn't bother picking up for me because she was real and honest and knew I wouldn't care, that we would get along fabulously. And we did.

That night, our girls danced together in matching pajamas and traded toys while I set up our temporary home in the coziness of Andy and Nici's downstairs bedroom that had been hospitably prepared for our visit with quilts and books and flowers. Nici gave me a tour of the house and, in her husband's art studio just an hour after we met, I went to sit down, missed the chair, and crashed to the floor, flailing my arms to catch myself. In attempting to save me, Nici reached out and accidentally grabbed my boob, and we both sank into puddles of laughter while Nici bravely admitted that she wet her pants a bit. Then we just sat there, half laughing, half crying, completely aware that this was one of those searing moments when you recognize all is as it should be. We laughed that it seemed we'd known each other for years—that it was wild and crazy how we loved each other so much and that our kids seemed to share our affection. And the entire week followed suit. We'd put kids to bed and retreat to the living room where the two of us stayed up until four in the morning huddled in quilts, sipping wine, telling stories, asking questions, laughing, crying, loving.

We reflected . . . a lot. About the past year. About the pain both of us had been through and how far we had come. Two months before Nella was born, Nici had spent a week in intensive care with her second daughter who, at two weeks, was on a ventilator grasping for life and fighting respiratory syncytial virus. I remember the desperate texts and the calls and feeling helpless for my friend who thought she might lose her baby. And little did I know then, she'd feel the same helplessness for me two months later.

"I'll never forget that call," Nici said late one night as we, once again, discarded the idea of going to bed for the chance of soaking up another hour of each other's company. She refilled my wineglass, then hers, and shifted into a more comfortable position, curling her legs underneath her on the couch across from me. I knew we were just getting started.

"I'll never forget calling you," I answered. And I remembered it clearly. The moment I sat in that delivery room, holding my girl, feeling the comfort of friends around me and yet wanting to tell my Montana friend who I knew was checking her phone every ten minutes for the news of our happy birth. I remember shaking while I dialed and waiting

for her to answer. I remember her exuberance, the smile I could hear in her voice when she picked up.

"Aaaahh! Is she here?" she asked breathlessly. And all I could do was cry, devastatingly, into the phone. I said it twice—"Nici, she has Down syndrome"—but knew she probably couldn't understand through my tears.

"Kelle, I never told you this," Nici said that night, "but my heart sank when I heard you. I thought she didn't make it. I thought you were telling me she died."

The two of us sat in silence. I fingered the stem of my wineglass and felt the grip in my heart, the hot tears on my face. No, she didn't die. Thank God, my girl didn't die.

"And when I realized what you had said, I was relieved she was, at least, here. But, oh babe, my heart hurt so badly for you."

We talked about everything that night and, yes, it included our pains, but mostly we talked about what we wanted to do with our wild and precious lives. I listened as her voice escalated with passion while she talked about her art, her kids, wanting to travel across the country with her family, writing, making things, and seeing the world. And she nodded and smiled as I told her all the places we wanted to visit, what I hoped my girls would learn, the people I wanted to meet. We retold childhood stories, listened, gave advice, and laughed until our sides hurt.

Andy, Nici's husband, got up with the girls—all four of them—the next morning and let me and Nici sleep. And when we finally pulled ourselves out of bed and trudged our way to the kitchen for coffee, we looked like hell but made it a point to say we'd do it again in a New York minute. Or a Missoula minute, which is a little slower, but quite lovely, I must say.

I'm so happy I schlepped my kids across the country and made that trip. My girls can now say they've picnicked next to a mountain creek and know what it feels like to watch clouds of dust kick up from our shoes on the Rattlesnake Wilderness Trail. I know the joy that comes from watching my girl hula-hoop in the mountain moonlight of a Montana vineyard, and I can say I took a leap and invested in someone I believed in, and she's become a strong part of my Net.

I came home feeling completely victorious again. Exhausted, but victorious. And I wanted to keep it going—I was hooked.

BUDDY WALK PREPARATIONS WERE QUICKLY UNDER WAY as soon as we returned home from Montana, and I was excited for the opportunity to publicly declare everything that was brewing inside my heart—the love for my girl and our family, the growth I had experienced so far that year, the enthusiasm for embracing our new challenge and transforming it into something good, even the pain that still rested in hidden parts of my soul.

Growing up in a Christian family, I was always taught that baptism was a symbol that represented an inward transformation. A dramatic dunking into water that sheds an old life and a refreshing emergence that signifies a new one. I've never technically been baptized in any faith other than having a wet rose stroked across my forehead as a baby, and I decided the Buddy Walk would be my grown-up baptism. A dramatic ritual that would epitomize our new life. We would gather friends, dress up, and march to the beat of life's pounding drum that called us to be more.

In creating a team name, I thought a lot about the theme of our year. I thought about what I used to chant to myself when acceptance was difficult—*I'm a rockstar, I'm a rockstar*—and the mentality I strived to in-still in my girls—that they could do anything, be anyone. So rockstars we became—a watered-down family version of the bat-eating tattooed

variety, of course—but still just as badass. I penciled "Nella's Rockstars" under the team name category on our registration form and quickly designed a fiery-flamed logo to go with it. If our Buddy Walk was going to be our baptism, it had to represent appropriately. My heart was full, and I wanted to show it.

"There has to be music," I told Brett one night as I folded team T-shirts and searched online for cheap studded leather bracelets.

"Kelle, I don't think they're going to have a deejay. It's a Buddy Walk, not a wedding reception." He'd grown accustomed to my far-fetched event dreams and prepared to reel me in.

"I know, but, babe, think about it. Music makes everything better. If there's music, maybe there will be dancing. And well, if there's dancing, it's in the bag. A huge, happy success. Music takes everything to the next level."

"It's a two-mile walk and we have a twenty-pound boom box in the garage," Brett suggested. "Will that do?"

I smiled. "Yes, that will do."

It did just fine, thanks to the most badass playlist in the history of humankind. We joined with friends and family at sunrise on the morning of the Buddy Walk and passed out Nella's Rockstar T-shirts as the boom box blared Baby O'Riley and Queen's Greatest Hits. Friends decked out in press-on tattoos, studded leather, and heavy eyeliner hugged and scooped up my mini Madonnas as we made our way to the starting line. And I cried as a high school choir sang the national anthem while I looked around at not only my own village but my community and the other families in our own town on this journey with us.

There was no blast of a gun to signal the walk had begun, just the happy procession of bodies—pulling wagons, hoisting little ones on shoulders. And we walked at our own pace because that's the way we do it in real life. As our group made our first strides, I watched my dad raise the twenty-pound boom box high over his head sending the triumphant tune of a Rolling Stone anthem echoing far ahead of us. "Let's rock!" he shouted.

We walked two and a half miles to those beats, along a stretch of boardwalk nestled between forest that filtered the morning light into a fan of sunshine, and when we returned back to the starting point, the music continued. Most families dispersed after they huddled to enjoy a few pieces of free pizza, but a few remained long after the walk ended and joined us in a small circle while we danced and cheered on the few kids who were busting a move and lip-synching Black Eyed Peas into Styrofoam microphones. It was a grand celebration, a hell of a baptism.

I realized that day, for the first time, that finally, Down syndrome meant something to me beyond my own girl. It was a part of my life, but I recognized it was a part of a lot of other people's lives too. And if it wasn't Down syndrome, it was something. I felt connected to everyone there in a way I hadn't in a long time, but I also felt guilty—ashamed that it took my own pain, my own connection to this new world to bring me here, to the larger picture. I wondered, if it wasn't for Nella, would I have even come had someone invited me?

I don't know the answer to that. Since Nella was born I have contemplated my own self-ishness and need to feel comfortable in life to the point that I could write a thesis on it. I've beat myself up, challenged myself, stretched my philosophy to see further, accept pain, open my comfort receptors to the vast degree of misfortune that exists in the world but ultimately thrusts us toward growth and understanding. The only thing I know is that something happened to us this year—something good

and unplanned and beautiful. And while I have vacillated between underrating its purpose and overanalyzing its existence, I have grown. I have embraced the world of difference as an opportunity to teach my family that life is rich and intricate and to be lived to the fullest—to enjoy, to give back, to learn, to teach. And, packing up our rockstar belongings and closing the boom box in the trunk that day, I felt thankful, even if it involved my own selfishness, for finally relating to a world that now embraced me.

I ONCE GOT IN AN ARGUMENT WITH ONE OF MY COLLEGE professors on this very topic. It was my first year of college, I was incredibly naive, and my philosophy professor most likely got off on confusing the young minds of college freshmen with his bait-and-hook-'em debates. He proposed that any act, no matter how philanthropic, was a selfish act. We, of course, the silly bullheaded freshmen, did the whole "Whoa, whoa, whoa" response, backing up our rebuttals with all sorts of scenarios. *What about anonymous givers? What about people who do good things having no relation to the cause?* But he, the cocky professor, proved us wrong every time. "Everyone does good things because it makes them feel good," he concluded. And there was no scenario I could think of to refute his final words even though I tried. Even Mother Teresa had to experience some sort of personal satisfaction from knowing she was helping the less fortunate. Their smiles and thank-yous had to serve as some form of reciprocation for her goodness. The argument made sense. In the same way, I put an end to the internal debate on my own selfishness. Does it really matter in the end? We're all in some way selfish beings, and the good of the world depends on that fact—that someone, somewhere will wonder what it might feel like to be in someone else's shoes, to feel their pain and, in doing so, attempt to do something about it. Our selfishness is ultimately what transforms us to be altruistic. And so, in the end, I accepted that my need to change how the world perceives *my* child is what fueled me to take the next step—to want to change the outcome of how the world perceives every child.

BY THE TIME HALLOWEEN ARRIVED, I FELT LIKE WE HAD nearly finished the prerequisites of our new special-needs parenting major, and we had matured at least into the sophomore stage. I hardly cried, seldom thought about Down syndrome, and was finally accustomed to rising above worries and fears. Occasionally, I'd question myself or wonder if I wasn't hitting the books as much as I should. The *New Parents' Guide to Babies with Down Syndrome* was completely blanketed in dust and hadn't been picked up—well, since Lainey found it one day in a moment of frustration and chucked it at Nella's head. Thankfully, she missed by a mile. Someone further along on this journey had shared with me one of the best pieces of advice I'd received, and that was put the books away, pull them out if I really needed to know something, and instead go buy a copy of the best resource I'd ever need . . . Dr. Seuss's *Oh, the Places You'll Go!* I may not have had it all figured out, but I confidently knew my position: I would proactively parent both my designer-gened kitten and my 46-chromosomed one as best as I know how, and that would entail a carefully crafted brew of research and instincts, but mostly just a wealth of love.

SOMEHOW, THE PAIN AND JOYS AND LOVE CRESCENDOED into gratitude and the grand satisfaction that we had arrived someplace better. We breezed through the festivities of both Halloween and Thanksgiving with neighborhood costume parades, afternoon baking sessions, trips to the beach, and late-night movies. And between the highs and lows of everyday life, I'd occasionally stop and wonder if perhaps we had healed too quickly—was there heartache around the bend or some hidden grief we hadn't dealt with? This self-doubt led to random therapy sessions with Brett after the kids were in bed. They were few and far between, but alike enough in nature to be generalized into the following script:

> Scene: Living room, dimly lit, where Brett sits comfortably on couch watching movie. Kelle walks in, wearing pajamas, bearing the concerned expression that informs Brett his sentimental wife is about to launch into a deep conversation involving feelings. Brett braces himself, turning down the volume and preparing for therapy.
>
> **Kelle:** "We're okay about everything, right? I mean, are you ever sad? Should we be sad?"
>
> **Brett:** "About what?"
>
> **Kelle (leaning in closer):** "Down syndrome."
>
> **Brett:** "What is there to be sad about?"
>
> **Kelle:** "I don't know. But do we need to talk about the future or anything?"
>
> **Brett:** "Do *you* need to talk about the future?"
>
> **Kelle:** "I don't think so, but you do realize it will probably get harder when she's not this cute little baby, right?"
>
> **Brett:** "Babe, she's our child no matter what. And we love her. We'll take one day at a time, just like we do with the boys and Lainey, and we'll be fine."
>
> **Kelle:** "That's how I feel too. So, you're cool?"
>
> **Brett:** "I'm cool."
>
> **Kelle:** "Turn up the TV."
>
> Curtain falls, applause.

And that's how it went. We live, we breathe, we reflect, we fall, we pick up, and we start over. We fell in early December when Nella contracted respiratory syncytial virus and spent a day in the ER where I held her while she was poked and x-rayed. I reflected on how blessed we were that this was not the norm, and yet I dwelled for a bit in the haunting land of "what if," because sitting in a hospital clutching your girl brings back all those increased likelihoods you forgot about. But here's the thing: once you become a parent . . . once you start feeling a little funny and you buy that pregnancy test . . . once you see a pink plus sign . . . once you know it's not just you anymore . . . well, you automatically carry around, for the rest of your life, an increased likelihood of having your heart broken. And it's a constant fear that we struggle to put to rest. We can choose to be afraid or we can choose to live. And I choose to live. Because an increased likelihood of having your heart broken also carries with it an increased likelihood of finding yourself the happiest you've ever been in life. And I was learning that when the "what if" voices came, I could tell them to shut the hell up and advocate for my child—attentively, fiercely, fully. That's where I was in the very last month of the year that rocked my world. I picked up. I attended to my family. And I was happy.

chapter 14

becoming real

OUR FAMILY RANG IN THE NEW YEAR ON A STARRY night with friends and neighbors slumped in beach chairs clustered outside in our driveway. We swaddled babies in our laps with heavy quilts as we watched the sky ignite with an exploding kaleidoscope of colors, and we cheered "Happy New Year!" at midnight as we kissed cheeks and clinked bottles. It was bittersweet for me—wrapping up every memory of the most meaningful year of my life and putting them away to become cherished relics in our family Hall of Fame. It also began a month of deep reflection on what it all meant—or, even better, what I *wanted* this year to mean. The end result is, ultimately, what we make of it.

Perhaps it's much ado about nothing—the bells and whistles of rockstar garb at a Buddy Walk, the hours of preparation planning decor and favors and festivities for my girls' birthday parties, the passionate need for me to return to the birth room to have some sort of purposeful moment of clarity and commemoration a year after that defining moment. Yes, I'm a bit of a ceremonialist, and the importance of these events is, in no way, made more or less by the presence or lack of attentive detail. But there's beige, and there's color. There's one life or one *wild and precious* life. We take efforts to make moments like exchanging vows or celebrating a high school reunion memorable and worthy of praise, and yet how many more events in our life are laudable occasions? I wanted to feel deeply the significance these moments played in my life story, and I was determined to celebrate them deservedly. Because once, a long time ago, I had a white picket fence, but it fell down. And while I didn't choose the crazy-colored one that was erected in its place, I had grown to love it. I wouldn't change it for anything in the world, and if there's one thing I've learned, it's that you can never *ever* go wrong with vibrant color.

Our vibrant color scheme unfolded as soon as I began making plans for the big day. I knew a few months before Nella's birthday that I wanted to do something extraordinary not only to celebrate such a memorable occasion, but to give back. We had felt so much support over the year, not only from our friends and family but blog readers and strangers who had reached out to help, and I somehow wanted to incorporate everyone in doing something that would benefit the special-needs community. The blog had naturally served as a tool to raise awareness for individuals with Down syndrome, and so I chose the National Down Syndrome Society (NDSS)—an organization dedicated to raising awareness and celebrating the extra chromosome—as the recipient of fund-raising efforts I would put together to honor our girl's first year.

I had no idea what to expect. My friend Pam at the NDSS helped me fill in an easy template as I set up our fund-raising website, and I hesitated for a moment when she asked me what my fund-raising goal was. It was three weeks before Nella's birthday. We had raised $6,000 for her Buddy Walk in October, and that was over a couple weeks' span, so I decided to pick a lofty goal and nervously typed *$15,000* in my e-mail to her with the explanation *"We're gonna go big."* Secretly, I was afraid she'd think I was arrogant.

I posted our fund-raising link on the blog along with several pictures of different individuals with Down syndrome I had acquired after an all-call I had put up on Facebook. I told my readers what I had learned that year and what I had gained from them and asked them to give back just a little—a suggested $5 donation to Nella's ONEder Fund.

We raised $15,000 in one day.

I don't know why I was so shocked. This year had already shown me how much good existed in the world and yet, really? $15,000? I was not only astounded by my readers' generosity but fueled to do more.

My friend Nadya—a fund-raising guru—and I were on the phone with each other every few hours after I initially posted. "Dude," she said after we raised our goal to $30,000, "I have a brilliant idea. $47,000. For 47 chromosomes."

"Seriously, you think we can do it?" I was so thankful for what we had already accomplished, I couldn't imagine it getting better.

"And what if we took your photo idea and went further? I'm thinking video." Nadya's like a wide receiver with a good idea. She can catch it, run it down a field, and score a touchdown like nobody's business. So we did it. I requested more photos and videos from my e-mail and Facebook connections within the Down syndrome community and Nadya stayed up until four in the morning dropping it into her movie software. Within two days, we had created an emotional video telling Nella's story and the hope for her future and all the other beautiful kids with designer genes. I posted it on the blog and asked others to spread the word. And then for the next two weeks, I watched the ticker on the fund-raising page jump higher and higher. By the thousands. Tears streamed down my cheeks as the screen blinked with donors' names. I didn't recognize most of them, but some I did—many of them familiar as blog commenters, friends from the past, family members, people who worked with my dad.

Someone I had never met donated $11,000. A friend of my cousin gave $1,000. And most of the rest was due simply to people who couldn't give a lot but wanted to give something. I will never again tell myself that my $5 can't help a cause because the outpouring of generosity of both strangers and friends raised, in three weeks, over $105,000 for Nella's ONEder Fund. Every one of our United States was represented, with donations from the North Pole to Key West, Florida, and over 350 donations came in from twelve different international countries as well. I was overwhelmed with gratitude and reminded that, if you look in the right places, you will find that the world is filled with so much kindness.

AS WEEKS TURNED INTO DAYS BEFORE NELLA'S BIRTHDAY, I was swimming in a lot of "where was I last year?" musings and, yes, some of those were painful knowing that blissful pregnant mama had no idea what kind of grief lay ahead of her. I remembered packing the diaper bag for the hospital, folding up the crocheted dress my mom had made for our yet-to-be-seen girl, falling asleep at night holding the taut skin that stretched across my middle where she kicked and somersaulted, promising we'd meet soon. It was painful and yet so very full circle to remember those flashes while holding Nella now, my beautiful girl who was very present outside of that once-round middle. My girl who waved and clapped and leaned across my chest while she was slung to my hip just so she could catch my attention and ignite my heart with her smile. How far we'd all come.

The week before Nella's birthday, I had a lot to do. One particular afternoon, I had laid Nella down in her crib for a nap and busied Lainey with a stack of cookie cutters and a ball of Play-Doh while I hurried

around the house tending to last-minute party planning and house-cleaning tasks. I stopped folding laundry (always receptive to an excuse to get out of it) when I heard the low hum of voices echoing from the baby monitor. Curious, I walked in the bedroom to find both girls, awake and giggling in Nella's crib.

"Her wanted me," Lainey explained, afraid she'd get in trouble. And I watched as Nella army-crawled across the crib sheet to get even closer to her sister, beaming when she succeeded to actually land in her lap, sprawled across Lainey's bent knees and reaching up to touch her face. They had a moment, my sister girls, locking eyes, giggling, lost in their own love language, and I, consequently had my own. A year earlier, I had wondered what it would look like—this sister thing—and grieved the loss of expectations I had acquired. Expectations much like this very moment. How silly I was to think they wouldn't love each other

in this way, that they wouldn't laugh or share a crib or speak their own sisterly language when the bond they held was far deeper and beautifully mysterious than I could have ever imagined. A year earlier, I had thought that our diagnosis required discarding all dreams of first-year milestones and breakthroughs, when really it delivered not only milestones but its own unique gifts—things like relishing the way her lower muscle tone allowed her little body to sink closely and comfortably into ours just like a flour sack or the way her crazy crooked army crawl and mad determination reminded us of a bloodthirsty roller derby girl and made us laugh adoringly. And, at nearly one year old, our girl matched her sister's enthusiasm, curiosity, and mad skills with her growing list of accomplishments. We celebrated milestones all right—and, boy, were they sweet.

By the time Nella's first birthday arrived, it was indeed an occasion to party, to celebrate, and to reflect. The theme was, appropriately, Bloom Where You Are Planted, and though I had spent hours setting up our yard with flowers and balloons and activity tables for kids, as it would go, South Florida picked January 22 for a gale-force wind day. So, bloom we did, indoors, where the house was in no shape for hosting guests— but it didn't matter. Bodies piled in, Brett lit a fire, friends found chairs and couches and ignored the fact that counters were heaped with last-minute preparation messes.

Kathleen, my ever-positive neighbor, piped up with her conclusion. "Kelle, it's just like the day she was born. You couldn't plan for this kind of weather, and you might be disappointed, but look around, honey. It's even better than you could have imagined." And it was.

At 4:22 P.M., I noticed the clock and realized in two minutes, it would mark the exact moment I laid eyes on her a year before. I wanted to be holding her. I wanted to whisper in her ear "Happy Birthday" and make up for the disappointment I experienced 365 days ago. I searched the crowd for my girl and found her in the arms of a friend where I ran to steal her. And I waited. Closed my eyes and squeezed her tight. A few more seconds . . . and then, 4:24 P.M. The room grew quiet as my dad said a prayer and tears ran down my cheeks as I felt her heavy head rest on my shoulder. I told her I was sorry I didn't welcome her the way I wanted to. I whispered "Happy Birthday" and "I love you" and "You are everything I ever wanted."

The day continued with cleanup and after-party laziness while I prepared for evening celebrations. Several weeks earlier, in another moment of attempted ceremonialism, I had e-mailed all the women in my life and called for a celebration of friendship on the night of Nella's birthday. Heidi had wanted to set up a late birthday party for me in January anyway, so it worked out perfectly to swap it out for something more important to me. The e-mail went something like this:

> Hi girls, in lieu of a birthday celebration this year, I really want you to come celebrate with me on the night of Nella's birth. The day belongs to Nella, but that night I want to celebrate life and be reminded of how one year ago, you were

all there for me. I want to celebrate YOU and the way women can empower, inspire, and lift each other up.

This circle of friends has grown over the years. As with any high-energy circle full of passionate women, there have been fallouts and misunderstandings, but mostly there is a whole lot of love. When the shit hits the fan, you truly recognize how much we mean to each other. I feel so lucky to know every one of you, and I want this night to be an opportunity for all of us to remember how important we are to each other. So, please come celebrate...

And then I upped the ante and told them all to bring one charm that represented their stories, their strengths, their words of wisdom that would be given to another woman that evening. We'd draw names and circle together and exchange charms that told stories of who we were and what we wanted our friends to know. I know, I know—a charm ceremony— how *Sweet Valley High* of us. I had a feeling it would work, though. I knew these women and their stories, and I had every confidence that summer camp kumbaya would be met with real, authentic female bonding, and our charm ceremony would go down in history as something to remember.

My cousins Joann and Emma—both of whom had flown down shortly after Nella was born—had returned to celebrate our big day as well as several girlfriends from out of town. All of them joined me, along with the rest of the girls, for a total of twenty-eight women who showed up that night—just as they did the year before. We walked into Lucarelli's Pizza and were met with the welcoming scene of candles and lanterns, heaping platters of bruschetta and roasted tomatoes, trays of bubbly drinks that were passed and refilled and later clinked together in emotional toasts that would not be forgotten. The Net was gradually assembling, its strong threads slowly finding their places for an epic evening that would strengthen our capabilities and reaffirm our purpose.

I had imagined all week what I wanted that night to look like—what I had hoped would happen, but one cannot plan these things, and calling everyone to pull their chairs into a circle and pass their charm to the left would have been far too forced—too *kindergarten-show-and-tell* or *sweet-sixteen-sleepover*, and I didn't want to screw with the fate of this evening's authenticity lest we end up pricking fingers and sharing blood. It couldn't be clichéd or cloying. No, this was far too special of an occasion. So I waited and watched as, organically, small circles of trivial chatter opened up and chairs slowly scooted and quilts were passed out and voices gradually hushed.

"Look, it's happening," Heidi whispered as a giant circle of bodies finally emerged.

"I know," I said, smiling. "It's just like I imagined."

I grabbed a fork from the table next to me and tapped it hard onto my glass to get the room's attention, not realizing it was inches from poor Joann's ear. Joann screamed and covered her ear and the room erupted with laughter. And then everyone stopped, turned to me, and waited.

What was I going to say? I had no idea. I stood there wondering how in the world one starts this kind of thing. There was so much I wanted to say, so many ways these women had given to me over this past year, and I didn't know how to give it back in one scratchy-voiced, heart-swelling speech. I scanned the circle—all twenty-eight women—and thought how

each had supported me this year. I stopped scanning when I saw Katie and Heidi, huddled next to each other. I met their eyes, and then closed mine, thinking of this very moment last year. They were there, sandwiching me and my girl so tightly in that hospital bed while I writhed and cried and begged for morning to come. They were stroking my hair and telling me this night would only be a memory someday—that they loved me, that it would get better and they knew it. And here we were, exactly one year from that night, and how my world had changed.

I went to speak but couldn't find my voice. Tears began to spill as love for every woman in that room took hold of me and the realization of my own journey sank in. One year. One year to that exact second in time that began as heartache and ended with such gratitude and love. I noticed my hands trembling and pulled them close to my side to make them still. I swallowed hard and leaned against Joann's chair next to me for comfort, looking out again to this sea of beautiful, capable, strong women who I knew and loved, and who loved me so fiercely, too.

"I just wanted to say," I cried, "that one year ago, I was curled into a fetal position during the saddest moment of my life and now, because of you—" I struggled to finish my sentence, my voice pitifully squeaking and pushing out a breathy, childlike whisper. "Because of you I am here, celebrating the happiest place I've ever been in life." I don't remember what else I said, but it had something to do with knowing that every one of us would need the Net someday and that I hoped everyone would feel it as I had when they needed it. I squeaked some more, attempted a joke to cut the tension of such concentrated emotion, and ended with some line about "We may all love our husbands, but sometimes we just need our girls."

"Amen," someone hollered, and the night continued with first one attempt at throwing names into a hat for the charm swapping and then another after we completely botched the first one, left out three people, and miscounted the group miserably. Somehow, the planets aligned the second time around as every woman who unrolled her chicken-scratched scrap of paper bearing the recipient of her charm seemed to have just the words the receiver needed to hear. We listened intently for hours, nestled under quilts that spread across multiple laps, refilling drinks, passing Kleenex, wiping tears as each woman expressed the meaning of her charm, retold her story, and shared regrets and hopes and words of advice. We laughed together at funny interjections that were offered right when we needed them most, and affirmed emotions with head nods and shoulder rubs or a good raucous "Cheers to that!"

Twenty-eight women shared that night. I surveyed the circle again somewhere in the middle of it and thought about every single one of my friends' stories. Several had yearned for children. Some had to wait too long. One lost a marriage. Many had miscarried. One had buried her child. One was undergoing chemo. Hearts had been broken; most had been restored. We had laughed with each other, cried with each other, offered our heartfelt support of "Hell yeah, he's wrong" and "No, she didn't!" or the most important "Hang on, I'll be right there." There had been fallouts and misunderstandings, lost friendships and regained ones—perhaps even awkward tension there that very night between friends who'd been hurt—and yet, all that put aside, we were there to support one another. To celebrate the more important event of showing up when we are needed. Because we are women, and with that comes spunk and vigor and the need to be heard and validated. With that comes the beautiful storm of strong opinions and the force with which we express them. There is pain. But, underneath, there is so much love. There is the need to answer a call when it comes, and that need and desire to hold each other up—it's truly a beautiful thing.

Twenty-seven charms later, I fingered the smooth silver of my own charms in my palm while I thought of what to say. I had chosen two charms because I couldn't decide between them—a small, round life raft and a shiny silver heart. Providentially, I had pulled my friend Theresa's name from the hat. Theresa, my friend who sent me the e-mail I'd never forget in the hospital the day after Nella was born. I suddenly remembered I had saved her words, tucked away in an e-mail folder I could never delete. I grabbed my phone and quickly scrolled through my folders until I found it and asked Theresa to read it aloud, knowing her words would be so appropriate to the theme of the evening and what I wanted each woman to know—that we were present for each other, that we were capable, and that we possessed the power to be there, come hell or high water.

Theresa took my phone and cleared her throat. "Dear Kelle," she began, "I'm at school trying to teach . . . I keep losing my thoughts as they return to you and your new little, Nella. This is odd for me, usually my thoughts are with my kids . . . but today they are with you and yours. Not only do you have my thoughts but you also have my heart and all the love in it. You need it more than I . . . keep it when yours is breaking, use mine to help repair yours . . . I trust you with it. I know that you'll return it when you no longer need it. I will leave you with my heart and thoughts . . . and try to teach. Today, because of you, I will teach: compassion, understanding, and love."

More Kleenex. There wasn't much more to be said except a few more *I love you*s and promises to lend hearts when the shit hit the fan for any one of us. We'd be there, just like we were tonight. We'd show up in birth rooms, at funerals, at parties, in the middle of the night if we had to, and we knew it. I made them all promise to remember that evening. To not wake up the next morning and embarrassingly regret opening up, crying, saying "I love you" even if a couple drinks propelled the courage to do so because what just happened was real and raw and meant to be remembered.

"Dude, you look like hell," Heidi offered. "No, seriously, your eyes are slits again and this is way too déjà vu. Would you go put some makeup on?" And we erupted with laughter, and soon the room shifted into a grand celebration where we danced and hugged and balanced the heavy emotion and puffy eyes with meaningful stories and really funny moments that can't be repeated (although my friend Donna does have a hell of a bikini wax story, let me tell you). It was, in a word, perfect. Perhaps the most full-circle moment in my life, where 365 days separated a sad girl in a dark room, out of breath, out of tears, and certain life would never be the same, from one who shamelessly belted out cacophonous choruses. One who victoriously celebrated life in a huddle of friends where we attempted to transform the back of an Italian restaurant into a lively dance club thanks to an iPod and my friend's husband, who handed her the keys to the restaurant well past closing and said, "I trust you. When you girls are finished, shut the place down." And shut it down we did, whooping and hollering "Tonight was awesome!" across the parking lot like frat boys who'd just scored, laughing at the trail of crap we had to haul out to our cars after our epic evening.

DAYS LATER, AFTER MY NEW CHARM WAS TUCKED INTO MY drawer and I had made the final twenty-minute trip to the airport to say the last good-bye, I returned home to shift gears, clean up messes, and recompose the companyless routine of where we had left off before Nella's birthday. While we were already weeks into the New Year, I felt it was just beginning—the page had finally turned and all the unfinished business of the past year completed. All, that is, except for one thing. I wanted to go back to her birth room.

I don't know why it was so important to me. It is, after all, simply a room. But just as walking into the purple-shag-carpeted bedroom of my childhood home or leaning against the yellow countertop of my grandparents' kitchen would, even after all these years, rouse latent emotions, I knew the birth room would do the same. It was the sacred setting of not only my most defining moment but my deepest grief, and if I had left any bit of my pain there, I wanted to return to face it. But mostly, I wanted to revisit the place I associated with so much sorrow and replace its memory with something good. I felt like I had made so much progress from the devastation I felt in that place, and yet I wanted to reconnect with it in a way that would bridge the gap between there and here, then and now, before and after.

My attempt to go back to the birth room was complicated. First, I scheduled a visit for the night before Nella's birthday and planned to include several girlfriends, but a full moon delivered a wild labor ward that night, pushing (no pun intended) off our plans until a few days later, and then later, and again, another try. Room 7 was very busy blessing other mamas with their new babies until finally, a week later, I called up and found out that the room was finally free. Suddenly, I was nervous, knowing that walking onto the sacred ground of Room 7 would reignite dormant emotions. Just thinking about it made those long-buried feelings stir within me.

Fortunately, two kindred spirits came with me—one who was so very present the night Nella was born, who remembers things even I don't, and one who wasn't, but wanted to hear the story from the place it started. So it was, Heidi and my beloved neighbor and friend, Kathleen, or Nana Kate as we call her, joined me for my journey to The Birth Room. I, in a moment of ceremonialism, scoured the house thirty seconds before we left, searching for divine totems from that night. The plastic Sharpie-scrawled champagne cups we used to toast her birth, the same candles that flickered when we welcomed her. I tossed them in my bag and settled for a bottle of Coors Light to bring to fill the cups because we had no champagne, and off we went.

There was pain—the searing beauty of it when we stepped into that place. It was brief but concentrated. Like I was standing in the room as a visitor at the edge of the bed watching my sad former self grimace and

cry. I could feel the emotion that was so present that night, and it hurt to revisit it. I felt such compassion for what my former self had gone through here and maybe even a little bit of guilt for how disappointed I had been—for how my girl's welcome included so many tears. We huddled, the three of us, for a small moment and cried—hugged it out and patted backs. And then, it left. The pain left the building, and it became a room where we celebrated. Where flowers gathered and friends smiled and girls sat at the end of my bed and told me she was the sweetest baby ever. I remembered the magic of that room very much like Room 10, three doors down, where three and a half years earlier I heaved happy sobs when Lainey's slippery little body was placed in my arms.

We popped the cork—or, in our case, twisted the cap—poured semi-cold beer into plastic cups—the same cups we filled just a year before—and toasted to the love that began in that room.

We told Nana Kate all about that night, remembering things we

almost forgot and marveling at how small the room seemed now.

"I swear the room was twice this size," Heidi said. Because what happened in that room seemed too big to fit into that space.

We lowered the bed, sat down, and told stories for an hour straight. And we laughed . . . a lot.

"Hey, remember this?" Heidi asked, and we turned to see her gripping the bedrail, heaving her head back and uttering some awful, guttural moan. She stooped over, erupted into laughter, and answered her own question. "Dude, that was you, dilated to, like, nine. That shit was awful." We laughed and spurred her on, and she obliged, telling more funny stories from that night—ones we had forgotten amid the sadness, and it was time they had their time to shine too.

"DID I EVER TELL YOU I GUARDED THE DOOR in the hallway like a Jedi knight, and if I saw anyone attempt to walk in looking sad or, God forbid, wiping a tear, I gave 'em a come-to-Jesus talk that there was no sadness allowed in Room 7? Swear to God, dude, I actually almost had to slap a couple faces. I told them 'You pull it together, you understand? We need to celebrate for Kelle. There is no crying in that room.' It worked too. Nobody cried." Heidi has a way of downplaying how she amazingly steps up to the plate as a friend. She has this hilarious self-deprecating way of telling stories that makes you heave with laughter but really, at that moment, I wanted to hug her and tell her, all jokes aside, there was no one I would have rather had with me that night.

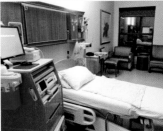

I left Room 7 feeling lighter, renewed and restored by the full-circle revelation that pain not only brings healing, but redemption. The faint light of a new moon guided me home that night, and while Brett had already put the girls to bed, I needed to be with them. I pulled Nella from her crib in the darkness, and the two of us joined Lainey in our bed so that I was sandwiched between them, calmed by the rhythm of their sleepy breath, sobered by the depth of my gratitude for their presence in my life. I kissed the smooth valley between their eyes—Lainey's, a deep dip that melted into the delicate bones of her tiny nose, and Nella's, an even plane of milky skin that puddled between the feathered swoops of lashes that framed her almond eyes. Both different, both beautiful. I whispered to them things I knew they couldn't understand but hoped somehow their souls would store for when they could. I told them they could do anything, be anything, and I'd love them just the same.

Brett finally joined us in bed and soon three steady rhythms of breath hummed around me until I too joined the chorus of sleep that night. The next morning we would stagger our wake-ups and stumble into the kitchen where we'd listen to the purr and trickle of the coffeepot, dig for lunch money for the boys, pour cereal for the girls, and begin again the healing rituals of both chaos and calm that fuel our life and propel us forward. No matter what, there's always a new day, a clean slate, an opportunity to begin again and vibrantly live out our "one wild and precious life."

A few days after I returned to the birth room, I felt such a sense of closure for our entire year, and I was happy to move on, to embrace the next horizon. In a last attempt to clean up unfinished business and remember once more the beautiful moments of a year I was now barely hanging on to, I went back one afternoon to a folder of e-mails I had saved from the weeks after Nella was born—comforting words, poems, stories, and prayers from friends and family as well as well-wishing strangers. Nella was asleep, and I turned on a rousing episode of *Dora the Explorer* to entertain Lainey while I combed through the old messages, rereading every one of them until I found one in particular I remembered—one that had comfortingly reassured me in those early days.

It was the tale of *The Velveteen Rabbit,* a book I had read to Lainey on many occasions, its most poignant and memorable words coming from the Skin Horse—the shabby old toy who shared the truth with the Velveteen Rabbit when he wanted to know what it meant to be real. The wise old Skin Horse, of course, told the inquisitive rabbit, who confused being real with being flashy and new, that being real is something that happens to you when you are loved. And when the rabbit asked if being real hurts, the Skin Horse answered honestly. He told the rabbit that, yes, being real sometimes hurts but that being real makes you not afraid of being hurt. In his final words to the innocent rabbit, the Skin Horse tells him that by the time you become real, you don't look so pretty. You

might not work like other toys or look as lovely but that it doesn't matter because when you are real, you can't be ugly.

I remembered crying when I had read that story after Nella was born, comforted by the greater truth that my baby girl didn't need to be flashy or look like everyone else to be real. But I realized something re-reading that story a year later—something I never thought to consider. The story of the Velveteen Rabbit was not about Nella. No, it was about me. For Nella was indeed very real from the start, but it was her mama who needed to be transformed by a greater love—a love that sometimes hurts. It was me who needed to become real, and in one soul-stretching year, I did.

I stared at the screen and began to read the story my friend had sent once more, but Dora was over and Lainey was hungry.

"Mama, make me some macaroni?" she asked, oblivious to my tears and pulling my arm toward the kitchen. I stopped and looked at the e-mail once more. "For Your Nella" the subject line read. I smiled for a moment and then rolled my mouse and clicked *delete*.

It was my story now, and I knew it by heart.

acknowledgments

I'VE ALWAYS PITIED THE POOR ACADEMY AWARD WINNERS who only get halfway through their thank-you speeches before the orchestra tunes them out and they are shooed offstage. I relate to them in that it's important to me that people feel recognized, and if gushing is what it takes—well, then let them gush. Thankfully, there is no conductor in this book and I will not be forced to fold my crinkled speech back into my tuxedo pocket and embarrassingly walk offstage.

Mrs. Kerspilo, my fourth-grade teacher, told me when I was nine years old that I was going to write a book someday. I, of course, had no idea I'd be so lucky to write a personal story of love and transformation, but I at least tucked her foresight as confidence somewhere in my subconscious. Thank you, Mrs. Kerspilo, for making me believe I could do anything. I hope my girls have teachers even half as inspiring as you were.

This book began in my head the day after Nella was born, but it became real when a couple months later Brett listened to my neglected voice mails and relayed that one of them sounded important. "A girl from New York who says she's a literary agent," he said. "Her name's Megan Thompson." Thankfully, I called Meg back, and it's one of the best moves I've made—yes, because she saw book potential in my emotional ramblings—but more notable because that day I inherited a dear friend. How a first-time author who knew nothing of the publishing world happened to score the most remarkable agent, I'll never know. I am deeply grateful for Meg's advice, experience, wisdom, and dedication to this book but mostly, for her friendship. Meg, we are so blessed that you are not just a part of the journey of this book, but of our real life story as well.

I knew the second I hung up the phone with editors Jessica McGrady and Cassie Jones at HarperCollins that they were my editing dream team. Special thanks to both of them for believing in a four-color photo memoir, for their brilliant expertise and fine-tuning, and for making me a better writer. This could have been an arduous process, but they made it both enjoyable and inspiring.

Special thanks to the incredible team at William Morrow: Liate Stehlik, Lynn Grady, Shelby Meizlik, Kimberly Chocolaad, Shawn Nicholls, Lorie Pagnozzi, Mary Schuck, Nyamekye Waliyaya, Andrea Molitor, and Laurie McGee.

I am deeply grateful for the guidance of Nadya Ichinomiya who listened to every chapter, pushed me to keep going, and reminded me of what this is all about. Her thoughtful advice was invaluable both personally and professionally, and I am thankful for a lifelong friendship that interestingly began over an odd combination of pickles and crackers on a plate. Nadya, thank you for helping me realize, as Shakespeare said, "To thine own self be true."

Thank you to Dr. Jennifer Foley who wrote the real epigraph of this story with her words "She's beautiful and she's perfect."

Thank you to the huge cast of loved ones and Naples Community Hospital staff who were present during our difficult time. You'll never know how healing your smiles, flowers, balloons, hugs, congratulations, and care were. You all made up for the welcome I couldn't give, and I am forever grateful to you.

Thank you to Heidi Darwish and Laura Cecil for taking the most beautiful birth photos a girl could ask for. You could have put the camera down when the emotion in the room shifted, but I'm so glad you didn't.

To the families and friends blessed with someone who rocks an extra chromosome or, for that matter, any special needs—thank you for welcoming us, supporting us, and providing countless resources for our family. You are a group of remarkable character and strength, and we have been inspired and encouraged by so many of you.

I know, I know, you hear the orchestra. I'm ignoring it. Moving on.

I owe a large debt of gratitude to my blog readers for supporting us with their kind words and readership. Thank you for believing in the half-full glass, for your generous gifts, cards, and e-mails, and for helping Nella's ONEder Fund to far surpass our goals. Thank you for sharing your stories as well and for allowing yourselves to be inspired and changed. And special thanks to Kleidy for her wisdom, encouragement, and countless moving quotes.

I cannot thank our friends enough for what they've been to us—a village of unfailing support. Thank you, Heidi and Katie, for the seven-hour hug during my night of despair. Thank you to everyone we're lucky to know who has embraced our new gift, loved our family, provided meals, sent cards, called, and extended support. And thank you for laughter—it is always the greatest gift.

Go ahead horns, keep playing. I'm not stepping off this stage quite yet.

Special thanks to Joann and Rebecca for flying in without hesitation. Thank you for watching *The Hangover* four times in a row and for making friendship so effortless.

To Dot and Nana Kate—my second mamas—neither of you hesitated for a moment to give my girl a celebratory welcome, and for that I thank you.

The Net—thank you. For happy hours at Hurricanes and more.

To Nici. Thank you for introducing me to Mary Oliver but more important, for living her poetry with me.

I am eternally grateful for the love and support of my friend, Heidi. Heidi, you should be cloned and sold as the world's greatest friend. It is amazing to have a friend really *get* you and you do just that. Thank you for living this book with me and for never ever failing to make my family feel loved.

To my family. Mom and Dad, because of you an extra chromosome is no big deal. You've both taught me that lemons are a gift—because the art of making lemonade changes you for the better. Thank you for your unconditional love and support and for never putting "perfect" on a pedestal. You both showed by example that the richness of life is often found in the less glorious imperfection of experiences that are interesting and soul transforming. Thank you for living creative lives and never settling for just *good enough*. Bubby, you are the best big brother and the one anyone would want with them when things get rough. Thank you for your humor and your love. And Carin, everything I've learned about facing hardship and being capable to handle it came from you. You are always the sister I look up to, the one I couldn't imagine life without. I love you.

Special thanks to my extended family—to Gary and Dahna, and aunts and uncles and cousins that ground me. And to the Hampton family—Brian and Donna, Roly and Colleen, Trish and Amy, thank you for your love and support.

To no one do I owe more thanks than to my husband, Brett. Thank you for supporting me through this book but mostly through life and raising our children.

Thank you to Austyn and Brandyn, the incredible gifts that came with my marriage. Thank you for loving and protecting your little sisters. And to Maria—I'm sorry I once called you the "old wife" because you are anything but an ex. You are a part of our family, and you were one of the first ones there with open arms to love Lainey and Nella and support us.

I've saved the most important gratitude for last, so please Orchestra, shut up for a moment. I want to be heard.

To my beautiful girls. For all the years I dreamed of being a mother, never could I have imagined the joy you would bring me. Lainey, you made me a mama, and I will never forget the way my world transformed with loving you. I hope you know someday just how much your pure and untainted love guided me through a defining year of my life. And Nella, little did I know holding you that day, while your tiny almond eyes blinked and begged me to accept you, just how you'd change our lives. Indeed, you've brought something extra to our family, and you've bonded us in beautiful ways. Both of you will forever be my most prized accomplishment and my greatest joy.

Now, while security drags me offstage, my last thank-yous are hollered out to the Isle of Capri, Mary Oliver, Sara Groves, Donald Miller, Florida sunsets . . . and extra limes.